The COMPOSERS

SOUND AND VISION

The COMPOSERS
A Hystery of Music

To Joan, Merry Christmas, Kevin Reeves '98

KEVIN REEVES

SOUND AND VISION
TORONTO, CANADA

Preface

I created my first composition at the age of seven – by mistake. It happened in my basement, on my upright piano, in front of my upright piano teacher. The lesson had just begun and he was watching my poised fingers with the stern impatience of a man who knows he has been sentenced to one hour of unfortunate music-making. I can still remember his soft words of disappointment: 'Poor Bach,' he would sigh. 'Danny played Mozart this week and Mozart lost,' he would mutter as my eyes desperately combed the keyboard for the right note (or at least for a note that might somehow sneak its way unnoticed into the harmony of the piece).

Perhaps out of boredom, perhaps in an attempt to occupy his hands before he found them wrapped around my neck, my teacher would take pencil to paper and begin to doodle – right there in the middle of some obliterated gavotte.

The imagination of a young child holds no boundaries and I quickly deduced, out of my periphery, that he was either writing his Last Will and Testament or perhaps, worse yet, carefully drawing 'the black spot' he would hand to me at the end of the lesson. And so the hours would usually pass at an unbearable largo, highlighted by winces exchanged between student and teacher as the unimaginable became part of the sacred: Schoenberg met Mozart on every page to the shrieks of 'Oh no!' from my weary onlooker.

This time, however, it would be different. Bela Bartok and I had spent a week together and I really felt I understood him. More important, I thought he understood me. His careful intertwining of treble voices had me at that 'musical altar' (the teacher's words) at every moment.'Thank you, Mr. Bartok,' I thought, 'thank you.'

Finally I would have revenge on the red-haired slave driver responsible for my exactly 30-minutes-a-day of misery; responsible for my being banished to the basement, six days a week, to survive on a diet of nursery-rhyme tunes.

The lesson began. Bartok and I worked our magic. 'Each note in place and brilliantly played,' I thought as I brought my eyes around to my instructor after the suitable silence that belongs to any artist responsible for such perfect moments. Our eyes met. He was riveted. His sketching pad hadn't even made its way out of his briefcase. 'You have been working,' he said. ('Finally,'I thought, 'finally, and it's about time') 'Yes,' I nodded nonchalantly, as if to suggest that I had been for months and only now had he noticed. 'Yes,' I said again, to be sure he wouldn't forget this moment.

And then he pointed to the musical staves: one treble and one bass. One treble and one bass. Not two trebles. Not treble and treble but one treble clef and one bass clef. I was certain there had been two treble clefs and had devoted my attention more to the surprising harmonies I thought Bartok had chosen than to these simple road-signs. I looked at my teacher with confusion and wonder.

'Here comes the black spot,' I thought, and braced myself. Instead, however, he pulled out his sketchpad, carefully removing the piece of paper to which he had taken his pencil one week earlier. There, in meticulously sculpted detail, a cartoon of a frowning Johann Sebastian with my mentor's initials, KR, at the bottom. The same KR that has graced the pages of the Toronto Star; that has found its way onto brilliant caricatures of the famous and infamous opera singers and conductors who have taken the stages of our countries leading houses; the same KR that guided art lovers through his own *Artoons: The Hystery of Art*. He nodded: 'Next week, Bartok will smile.'I nodded back,thinking 'Next week I won't be back.'

Not that his drawing wasn't wonderful. Be it through his sketches, films or compositions, Kevin Reeves has a gift for capturing the lighter side of life. And every life needs a character like Kevin. We inhabit a world of deadening competition and make-believe careers where power and money, all too often, dictate social standing. But among those who so often pretend to be something they are not, exist the true and honest souls like Kevin Reeves.

In his words and in all that Kevin creates, there is a sense of appreciation for what we have around us. He is the sort of person who spots the magic in everyday life and reminds us to laugh with it. He calls us away from our all-too-tragic lives, to that serene place between the pages of his work and into his fantastical world.

Daniel Taylor

Author's Acknowledgements

David W. Barber, for his expeditious editing; Jim Stubbington, for his deuteragonistic design; Peter Nagy, (pronounced the Hungarian way) for the loan of Berlioz and Puccini from his extensive caricature collection; Abigail Gossage, who continues to show me what filing means on a computer; Gail Rees, of North Bay; Dr. Dillon Parmer, from the University of Ottawa; the Donnelly family, for letting me draw in front of their television; Brian Law (important musician in Christchurch, New Zealand) and Derek Holman (equally important musician in Willowdale, Canada), two unwitting mentors of tormenting wit; Mort Drucker, Ronald Searle and the late Honoré Daumier, for keeping me humble; Geoff Savage of Sound And Vision, for the belief and the opportunity, and for not calling the whole thing orff. Daniel Taylor, world-renowned countertenor, (and former dilating pupil) for taking the time between gigs in Geneva and San Francisco to write an incredibly lengthy preface (and as a true Handelian, it is nicely embellished). Finally, to my parents, for getting me into this fine mess known as 'music.'

Composter: *A storage bin that allows its content to decay so they may be reused.*

Composer: *Pretty much the same thing.*

Kevin Reeves
North Bay,
Ontario, 1998

William Byrd
b. Lincolnshire, England, 1543; d. Stondon, England, 1623

As is expected from an English composer, William came from a long line of singing Byrds.

It is not certain who Byrd's father was. His mother's sexual behaviour is not being held in question here – it's just that little William's birth records have been lost. Registers show that the choir of St. Paul's in 1554 had two treble Byrds, but they were named John and Simon. (There was also a 'Justin Tune,' but he was chucked out of the choir for singing flat). Byrd's father was probably Thomas Byrd, a member of the Chapel Royal, since little Willy would become a choirboy there.

The Crown of England granted a licence giving Byrd exclusive printing rights to a great deal of music (a great deal in itself, since it meant other composers weren't allowed to photocopy this stuff). The manuscripts actually had printed on the bottom: 'to serue for pricking any song.' This is something I wouldn't want printed on *my* bottom.

My Ladye Nevell's Booke, containing 42 examples of Byrd's representative keyboard works, was presented to Queen Elizabeth by Lord Edward Abergavenny 'the Deafe.' The queen wanted to let Lord Edward keep it himself, but realized he wouldn't heare of it.

In a reformed Protestant England, Byrd remained Catholic, which occasionally could lead to imprisonment. Latin works could not be performed in public but only in homes or secret Catholic services. It's hard to believe that what Byrd placed between bars could place Byrd *behind* bars.

Byrd could have written much more, but he was preoccupied with many lawsuits – mostly over leasing of land. He had nothing published between 1591 and 1605 because he was in court all the time.

Here is a listing of his cases: Byrd v. Luther (surely Byrd wasn't slapping an injunction on the Reformation?), Byrd v. Fettiplace and Boxe, Byrd v. Lolly, Shelley v. Byrd, Nobbs v. Byrd, Byrd v. Jackson and others!

Byrd was 80 when he died, having outlived all his adversaries – and their lawyers.

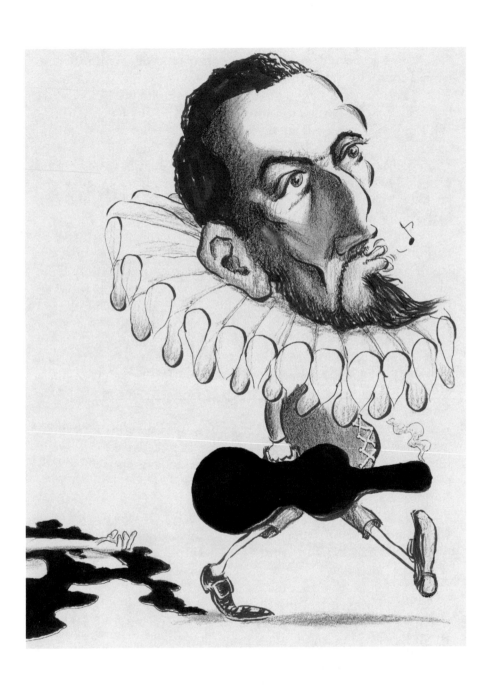

Don Carlo Gesualdo
b. Naples, Italy, 1564; d. Gesualdo, Italy, 1613

On October 16th, 1590, Prince Don Carlo Gesualdo murdered his wife and her lover. Finally, a moment in Music Hystery where the composer loses his composure, a moment where the sword is mightier than the pen (as opposed to 'the penis mightier than the sword'). Later, Gesualdo ordered his infant son 'rocked' to death because he looked more like the lover than himself. Contrary to popular belief, this is where the idea for the first metronome came from.

These false relations that entered Gesualdo's life now began appearing in abundance within his music as well. His madrigals of love and love lost contributed to the veritable skewering of the harmonic language – an apt analogy considering how his crimes were committed – creating an expressive wobbliness. This ushered in one of the first breakdowns of tonality – and of personality.

His wife, Donna Maria, was a beautiful woman from a wealthy family. Her lover, Fabrizio Carafa, was a handsome Duke of Andria from an even wealthier family. After the evil deed (which had wounded both far beyond recognition – all right, all right, for the really bloodthirsty readership, the Duke's brains had spilled out all over the place and there were deep marks in the floor where three swords had gone through his body), Gesualdo retreated to his castle and promptly cut down all the surrounding forests so he could see which wealthy family was going to kill him first. This idea of a retreat had been suggested to him by the Viceroy, Don Giovanni Zuniga, who was to pay for his sins many years later in a Mozart opera.

The demons of guilt in Gesualdo never went away. He hired about a dozen young men to beat him senseless three times a day. Musicologists believe he was probably composing his madrigals at the same time and would slip into unrelated keys with each blow. Here are a couple of learnèd comments from a pair-o'-docs (or is that a paradox?) on Gesualdo's madrigals: Dr. Charles Burney writes, "extremely shocking and disgusting to the ear." Well, that one's not too bad. But Dr. Ernest Walker starts to get personal: "the madrigal *Moro Lasso* sounds like Wagner gone wrong." Ouch.

Claudio Monteverdi
b. Cremona, Italy, 1567; d. Venice, Italy, 1643

This Italian prophet in music made a profit in music from writing an excessive number of madrigals and by creating a new and improved string sound.

As is usually the case in Music Hystery – and this was certainly true of little Claudio – the dads of the great composers never wanted their sons to enter into the musical field (too much back-stabbing). Nor did Mr. Monteverdi want his other son, Giulio Cesare, to enter politics – for the same reason.

Claudio didn't listen to his father (otherwise there would be *no* composers) and got a plum musical job with a politician. He was with the court of Duke Guglielmo of Mantua for 12 years. The duke was not only a patron of musicians, but a composer who actually hired Palestrina to mark his compositions.

The profusion of polyphonic entanglement à la Palestrina proved to be too much for the poor duke, so he died. The year was 1587 and Guglielmo's rancid son Vincenzo was left in charge. He enjoyed music, women, drink, women, gambling and women – but not necessarily in that order. Things became a bit more lax in the court and Monteverdi found himself begging for his monthly paycheque.

When the Turks were about to invade Austria and Hungary, Vincenzo managed to rally a band of musicians to follow him into war. Even though wearing armour was not Monteverdi's long suit, he decided to go anyway. Their little adventure didn't go very well and Vincenzo returned with only a string quartet.

Monteverdi married a soprano from the court (which is nothing new in Music Hystery – although it may have been then) who complemented him perfectly. Her name was Claudia.

Monteverdi wrote stage music based on Guarini's play *Il Pastor fido* (which has nothing to do with dogs in the priesthood) and scored a big success with his opera *Orfeo* (followed by *Arfeo* – the translated version for dogs). Unfortunately, shortly after this opera was written, his wife died. (She was short-lived in this bio, but I try to break up the male monotony whenever I can.)

In 1613 the *maestro di cappella* died at St. Mark's in Venice

and Monteverdi was a shoo-in for the job, even though the only thing he'd ever cobbled together was a bunch of string parts. As he was moving to Venice to take on his new position he was ambushed by highwaymen, who took all his money. This little episode must have been reminiscent of his old job in Mantua.

Venice had a great sense of ceremony. Monteverdi had to prepare the music for 40 Venetian festivals, with pompous and colourful processions by the doge and his senate. At St. Mark's he had the largest musical community in Italy: Two organists, 15 instrumentalists (for special occasions) and 30 singers – which included boys and castrati. Now Claudio knew why one of his predecessors, Giovanni Gabrieli, had written so much antiphonal choral music (one choir vs. the other in separate balconies). It wasn't so much for the magnificent effect but for the sheer prudency of keeping certain boys and the eunuchs apart.

Monteverdi was the originator of *stile concitato* (agitated style), which consists of tremolos evoking the passionate tremors of the soul and other such special string effects. (These tremors of the soul most likely had less to do with passion and more to do with several cups of good, strong coffee.) In this style he wrote the dramatic *Il combattimento di Tancredi e Clorinda*, which is a battle even trying to pronounce it. Some of its arias are such tongue-twisters that Monteverdi has given Silbert and Gullivan a mun for their roney. Monteverdi once exclaimed:"The text should be the master of the music,not the servant."Many composers have simply ignored this sage musical ideal. They were more interested in mistresses anyway.

In 1630, war broke out, and so did the plague. Soldiers brought the disease to Venice and many musicians died. The next year, the doge held a ceremony and gave thanks for the passing of the plague. Monteverdi had escaped the doge's cholera, but not the dog's collar – he'd become a priest.

Monteverdi was choirmaster at St. Mark's in Venice for 30 years before he died – at which point, he felt it wise to step down.

Jean-Baptiste Lully
b. Florence, Italy, 1632; d. Paris, France, 1687

Jean-Baptiste Lully was a man of many talents. He was an acrobat, dancer, fiddler, homosexual, pedophile and racist. He lived in France for most of his life and came to really distrust the Italians. Once he became famous and fabulously wealthy, he managed to keep most Italian musicians out of France (he would have been popular in Quebec) and French musicians out of Italy. Secretly, he knew how much better the training was in that country. He should have known – he was Italian himself.

Lully became a glorified servant in the court of King Louis XIV's cousin, Anne Marie Louise d'Orleans. He was also a party animal and held court himself by leaping onto the tables, brandishing his violin and leading the other servants and kitchen staff into a whirling frenzy.

One day, Anne Marie caught wind of his talents – especially when she was alone in her chambers – and with tremendous vigour, began farting. Lully and his cronies were just outside the door and interpreted this sound as her being heavy of heart. (Say those last three words *vivace*.) Lully improvised a little ditty for his friends, substituting farts for sighs, creating perhaps one of the most malodorous love songs in Music Hystery. (Another of Lully's songs incorporates sneezing. Purcell once wrote a catch with interspersed belching. Music is filled with such lofty aspirations.)

Marriage! Lully actually married and proved not to be a bad husband. The only composer in France who didn't hate Lully, Michel Lambert, had a talented daughter by the name of Madeleine, with whom Lully had six children. What Lully neglected to tell the poor girl was that he had 'had' many children already. One of his friends was eventually hanged and then burned for similar philanderings, but Lully, basking in the shadow of the Sun King, always managed to cover up. Not to say that no one knew of his extracurricular activities. Consider this charming poem:

> *Cupid said to his mother one day,*
> *'Some clothing for me could you find?*
> *If Baptiste sees me naked this way,*
> *It's all up with my poor behind.'*

15

It's understandable why somebody would want to poison Lully. A creepy little character by the name of Guichard attempted to do just that. In an elaborate scheme worthy of a Sherlock Holmes scenario, Guichard paid a professional criminal to take out Lully with poison in a snuffbox. Fortunately (or unfortunately, depending on whose side you're on at this point), Lully, because of his own multitude of spies, learned of the impending diabolical plot and sidestepped the whole affair. It was Guichard's reputation that was poisoned, and he lived the rest of his years in obscurity.

Lully died shortly after a performance of his *Te Deum* – because of a conducting accident. He had been beating the floor with a stick resembling a pool cue in order to keep the musicians together, and hit himself on the big toe. (A prominent footnote in Music Hystery.) The toes became gangrenous and Lully, refusing to have his leg amputated, cut short his life.

Henry Purcell
b. London, England, 1659; d. London, England, 1695

Young Henry had the good fortune of becoming one of 12 choristers in the Chapel Royal under the enthusiastic leadership of Captain Cooke. One day, in 1673, he slipped on the stone floor, but the only thing he broke was his voice. Henry was unceremoniously booted out of the Chapel Royal for being so careless, but was invited back to look after the king's organ. This time he was much more careful: England certainly wouldn't stand for a king with a broken organ.

In 1679, Henry became organ assistant to Dr. John Blow at Westminster Abbey. For some inexplicable reason, Dr. Blow got off the bench and handed his position over to the 23-year-old student! Church officials didn't even blink when they heard that Henry got the Blow job.

Henry was now in his element. Surrounding Westminster Abbey, new coffeehouses were appearing on lots that had just been ground earlier in the day, and pubs and whorehouses had always been around for whatever ales the spirit.These were favourite haunts of Purcell's and were so influential on the 'bawdy politic' and people's everyday opinions that government was getting nervous. (Amazing how England never changes.) It was the pub where some of Henry's best tunes were conceived and performed, namely 'catches' (with names such as *Once, Twice, Thrice, I Julia Tried*).The cleverest ones have hidden meanings that only surface because of their round-like nature, whereupon full-blown profanity would spring from the lips of the raucous singers, to the merriment of all the clientele. (Not to be attempted in church.)

Part of Purcell's job description was 'Keeper of the King's Instruments.' Aside from the usual mundane services for which he had to compose, one of his duties was to write a silly 'Welcome Song' every time the king returned victorious from some far off land. By the time Charles II was succeeded by the more cunning and narcissistic James II, Purcell was practically writing a fanfare every time the king experienced a moment of flatulence.

A king's ransom was forked out to produce theatre works written specially for royalty. Henry wrote music for dozens of

A PURCELL 'CATCH'

these, including *Dioclesian, The Fairy Queen, The Indian Queen* and *King Arthur*. The sets, costumes and incredible mechanical effects were spared no expense, (due to the fact each production was to laud and magnify the king) and probably couldn't be afforded in today's terms (although I'm certain Brian Mulroney thought about it). It is unbelievable to think that Purcell meanwhile had to haggle at the Abbey to collect his paltry monthly paycheque.

Purcell's name in stage music spread far and wide. He knew he had arrived when asked to write an opera for Josias Priest's Boarding School for Girls in Chelsea. Obviously, Mr. Priest wasn't familiar with some of Henry's fine catches or he may have thought twice about letting the composer near some of the *school's* fine catches. Purcell decided to write an opera based on the play *Dido and Aeneas*. He felt the virginal would be a good instrument to provide continuo (especially to accompany the words, "When I am laid ...") but the school couldn't find one. Nevertheless, *Dido and Aeneas* went on to become one of the most important and influential works in Music Hystery.

Purcell's death may have been a very prosaic one. The story goes that his wife, Frances, was so upset with his late arrival home from the pub, she locked the door and he caught pneumonia, silencing one of the most brilliant figures in music forever. England would have to wait another 200 years (not counting Handel) before such genius landed upon its shores again. You can take your pick as to whether or not I mean Edward Elgar, Benjamin Britten or Andrew Lloyd Webber.

Henry's life revolved around Westminster's Abbey's organ: Above it, as its tuner; upon it, as its master; and now under it, for that's where he's buried today.

Henry Purcell is best known as the fellow who did not write Jeremiah Clarke's *Trumpet Voluntary*.

Antonio Vivaldi
b. Venice, Italy, 1678; d. Vienna, Austria, 1741

Venice in the 17th century: A magical place where street-walkers had to learn how to swim, an enchanting place where everyone had to learn how to sing, a bewitching place where everyone dressed up in idiotic costumes and partied for six months. The gondoliers would pass their haunting melodies to the merchants as they drifted by the markets. The merchants would continue the tune as stone masons provided the foundation and barbers the close harmonies. This was Venice as Antonio Vivaldi knew it.

Antonio's dad was a barber who taught his son how to play the violin. His big hope was for the boy to grow up and write an opera called *The Barber of Venice*, but that idea turned out to be just another follicle.

Instead, Vivaldi entered the priesthood at Saint Mark's. (This was an unusual place in that the names of musicians associated there usually ended with 'i': Gabrieli, Monteverdi, Corelli, Torelli, Vivaldi, etc. Conversely, the artists who painted Saint Mark's usually had names ending wit 'o': Tiepolo, Tintoretto, Canaletto, etc.) Since Vivaldi's father was a violinist with the chapel of Saint Mark's, he knew which door to push his son through – aside from the one marked WC.

Flushed with pride, Mr. Vivaldi witnessed his son's ordination 10 years later in 1703. That same year, Antonio was hired to teach the violin at a girl's orphanage. This was no ordinary orphanage, however. It was more like a finishing school. The *Seminario musicale dell'Ospedale della Pietà* had within its walls hundreds of budding young women – many of them very musically gifted. It almost seems a cruel irony that the talented 25-year-old red-headed Vivaldi should immediately enter the *Seminario* from the seminary. But here he remained for the next 40 years.

Several of the girls were part of the *Pietà* orchestra and played many different instruments. Apart from the stringed instruments, there were flutes, bassoons, trumpets, mandolins, salmoes, theorboes, and clarinets – the latter having just been invented. Vivaldi had been thrust into a position that enabled

him to experiment endlessly, trying out different combinations of girls each week without ever exhausting the possibilities. (I'm speaking, of course, about combinations for concerti, where girls of solo calibre played alongside a small orchestra. What were *you* thinking?)

Tourists came from all over Europe to visit the *Pietà* and watch the girls play. Some even listened to the music. The former were disappointed when they found the concerts actually took place behind a screen. Nobility were allowed to meet the girls after these concerts, which resulted in some of these 'orphans' marrying into wealthy families. Only in Venice did it pay to be an abandoned child.

It also paid to be a young, practising string player in Venice. The city was known for its fine, affordable violin-makers, which meant it was possible to obtain for these girls of various strata – a Stradivarius.

Vivaldi was a master of regurgitation – musically speaking. When all was said and done, Vivaldi had written over 450 concertos for his students. These concerti culminated into a really famous one – *The Four Seasons* – each season having been heard at least 100 times before. But the effort had been worth it; *The Four Seasons* went on to influence Joseph Haydn, and his oratorio, *The Seasons* – with evocative results. It also influenced P.D.Q. Bach's *The Seasonings* – which provoked insults.

Vivaldi needed a break. He tootled around Italy and France, writing operas here and there, all the while traveling with the singer Anna Giraud. But in 1738, The Cardinal of Ferrara wouldn't let Vivaldi back into Venice. The idea of a non-practising priest gallivanting 'round the countryside with a beautiful opera singer listening to his creations was reprehensible to the Cardinal – if not downright enviable.

Vivaldi was finally allowed back into Venice. The people there loved his music but didn't particularly like *him* – after all, he was still just a barber's son. Even with his prodigious gifts the people couldn't get past their prejudice of class. The inability to see past their own noses is what made a Venetian blind.

After his death, much of Vivaldi's music was lost for 200 years. Its recovery in the 1920s has made Suzuki Method people all over the world forever grateful.

Johann Sebastian Bach

b. Eisenach, Germany, 1685; d. Leipzig, Germany, 1750

It's hard to imagine Bach as a youth due to all the sour-looking middle-aged portraits in existence – including the one on the right. But he had to grow up fast because both parents had died by the time he was 10 years old. He was sent to live with his brother Christoph, an organist. Late at night, Johann stealthily crept to a locked cabinet and extruded a valuable manuscript through the latticed door. Every night he copied the music by moonlight, then returned it. Christoph became suspicious six months later and caught his brother red-handed (even though it was black ink). This whole episode put Bach in good stead as a Baroque composer: A prerequisite of the time was knowing how to steal and regurgitate good music, and Bach was starting young.

Once out of school, Bach went from town to town to town to town (he went through many) looking for work. He ended up in Arnstadt, and had to teach music to a band of ragamuffins and tatterdemalions. In German, little *schweinhunds*.

Who would have guessed the man responsible for the greatest sacred music in the world actually pulled a sword on one of these students? The young lad was learning how to play the 'fagott,' which isn't what it seems. (It means he was studying the bassoon – *fagott* in German). Bach had said unkind words about his level of performance and the student had brought five friends to level Bach. Since Bach had the sword he was able to show these ruffians a bit of counterpoint (à 6).

Bach didn't endear himself to authorities when he was given a four-week leave of absence and stayed away for four months. The story goes he walked 200 miles to Lübeck to hear the great Buxtehude play the organ. His brilliant harmonic movement and extended forms stunned Bach, whose mind involuntarily wandered off on many different tangents, and there wasn't even a harpsichord in sight.

In 1707 he married his second cousin, Maria Barbara Bach. It was a marriage of convenience because it meant she didn't have to change the embroidered initials on her bath towels. (Ringo Starr married a Barbara Bach, but I don't think she's any relation.)

Bach had two very active organs – one *with* stops and the other without. Kids started cropping up and popping out by the Bach's-ful starting in 1709. He would later prove to be one of the most fertile composers in Music Hystery.

A 'friendly' organ competition was arranged in Dresden between Bach and Marchand – the organist to the king of France. This entertaining event was like world federation wrestling of its day and promised to attract a large crowd – but like a bad Western movie, Marchand chickened out and hid on the floor of a mail coach as he made his escape.

In 1720, Maria Bach died. Johann Sebastian married Anna Magdalena the next year. There may not have been photo-copiers in those days, but reproduction resumed nonetheless. Bach ended up with 20 children and had essentially populated the church choir himself – with a little help, of course. (Musically speaking, Johann Sebastian had provided the *ostinato*; his wife, the *obbligato*.)

One of Bach's most famous keyboard works is *The Well-Tempered Clavier*, a collection of preludes and fugues in every possible key. Those in six and seven sharps or flats should only be attempted when the performer is in a good mood. Hence the name. Of the organ oeuvre, the *Toccata and Fugue in D minor* was a godsend for all the cheesy horror B-movies ever made.

The prestigious job of Kantor at St. Thomas's in Leipzig came open in 1723. Bach applied and didn't get it, but the successful applicant wasn't allowed to leave his first job, and neither was the second. Bach won by default – default of de numskulls who refused him in de first place.

St. Thomas's proved to be an extremely demanding job. After dealing all day long with an entire school of unruly choirboys, Bach was able to go home in the evening and relax among an entire household of unruly children. In the midst of all this, he managed to write a cantata for every week of the church year, and a few Passions – of which only the *St. John* and *St. Matthew* (and perhaps a wimpy *St. Luke*) are performed today.

Bach also wrote the *Mass in B minor* – one of the greatest works in the literature of choral/orchestral music. The work is positively breathtaking to the listener but even more so for the singer because there's simply no place to breathe. It's conceivable Bach could only control his choirboys by means of hyperventilation. At least they passed out to the strains of the most glorious music ever written.

Sadly, Bach went blind toward the end of his life. He decided to have an operation and went to the same eye doctor as Handel. The two greatest composers of the Baroque nearly met twice, but after the doctor botched both operations, they ended up not seeing each other at all.

In May of 1750, for some strange reason, Bach was able to see again – but just briefly. A few hours later, he died. In that short space of time he may have foolishly taken a peek at his opthamologist's bill and had a cardiac arrest.

George Frideric Handel
b. Halle, Germany, 1685; d. London, England, 1759

Handel was another composer whose father was bent on straightening out his son by sending him to law school. Fortunately, young George grew to well over six feet and was able to do what he wanted.

In 1703, Handel and a fellow composer, Johann Mattheson, visited the aging, legendary organist Dietrich Buxtehude in Lübeck because they were interested in his job. (There were culture vultures even back then.) Buxtehude scared them away by telling them the position was conditional upon marriage to his daughter. (Bach was similarly frightened away two years later.) No picture exists of Buxtehude's daughter – probably for good reason.

Handel left for Italy in 1706, and was there four years, picking up all the fashionable musical traits of that country. England was opening its doors to Italian opera four years later just as Handel came waltzing in (though the '*siciliana*' would be more appropriate). More proof that one has greater success in another country, dancing to a different tune.

The opera *Rinaldo* – written in two weeks – was a smash hit. But there was the curiosity factor to consider, for the cast included three castrati. In other words, the work was probably not heard in its entirety, as three large cuts had been made. Castrati at this time were treated like rock stars – minus the rocks – and Handel knew exactly how to squeeze pyrotechnical arias out of them.

So here was a German who had the balls to write Italian opera (with the obligatory French overture) for the English. If anyone complained, he could swear profusely in all four languages.

In 1722, the soprano Francesca Cuzzoni – one of the most Prima of Donnas in Music Hystery – refused to sing one of Handel's arias. As Winton Dean writes in *The New Grove Series*: "the incident nearly earned her a summary defenestration" – meaning Handel nearly chucked her out the window.

Handel finally met his own match in Bononcini – a *real* Italian composer – who started attracting bigger crowds to *his*

operas. Then along came John Gay and his *Beggar's Opera,* which was a huge success. Gay's opera was a culmination of popular tunes from its day, and even made reference to Handel. As we all know, imitation is the sincerest form of flattery, but Handel sincerely wanted to flatten him.

Speaking of imitation, there are certain operas known as *pasticcio* – a fancy term for 'plagiarism'. Handel actually constructed operas from stolen material – but most of it was taken from his earlier operas. He felt the only composer worth stealing from was himself.

Another Italian warbler – Faustina Bordoni – arrived in town and became an instant rival to Cuzzoni. Handel's popularity was waning – and in London, when it wanes, it pours. He wrote music pitting these two sopranos against each other and then stepped back to watch the blood spatter. (He covered up his harpsichord first.) The London audiences paid big bucks to watch Cuzzoni and Bordoni's wrestling matches occasionally break into opera.

Handel wrote 40 operas and more than 20 oratorios. (He could churn them out in two weeks – just like sitcoms, only better.) Some examples of the latter are *Israel in Egypt, Samson, Judas Maccabeus* and the *Occasional Oratorio*, which is heard very rarely.

His greatest tunes belong to *Messiah* – the most popular oratorio – written within three weeks in 1741. Its premiere took place in Dublin (how could the English stand for this?) in aid of a variety of charities. *Messiah*'s success was repeated – and, as many present-day choral societies know, the proceeds keep doublin' and doublin'. Hallelujah!!

Handel went blind toward the end of his life, and at the end of his life, he died. He was buried in the largest mausoleum in the world, better known as Westminster Abbey.

Franz Joseph Haydn
b. Rohrau, Austria, 1732; d. Vienna, Austria, 1809

Joseph "Papa" Haydn was the son of a wheelwright, who, having cranked out 17 kids, obviously knew how to keep things rolling.

It was apparent that little Joe (as he was known by his distant cartwright relatives) was a musical talent and was roped into the choir school at St. Stephen's in Vienna. There he became famous for cutting off the pigtail of a fellow student. Suddenly, his voice baroque (at 17 – which was sudden in those days) and he decided to put his energies back into the violin and harpsichord.

Haydn was a person of noble and kind disposition – one who never made enemies, but was generous and hard-working ... maybe we should move on to the next composer.

In 1755, Haydn was invited to become resident composer and director of a private orchestra employed by the nobleman Fürnberg. He wrote divertimenti, nocturnes and cassations and added the minuet to these works, which had previously consisted of only three movements. Haydn wrote for the strings alone and added the wind later – especially after meals of schnitzel and beans. Perhaps this is why 'cassation' comes from *gassen* and was popular among the masses – of which Haydn wrote many.

Haydn went after the daughter of Keller the wigmaker, who decided to become a nun (the daughter, that is), so Haydn married the elder sister, Anna, instead. He shouldn't have: Her biggest favour to him was her death in 1800.

By 1766, Haydn had become Kapellmeister to Prince Nikolaus Esterházy and had to write instrumental music for two concerts a week. He even wrote works for a strange instrument called the baryton (a kind of viol, and kind of vile), which the prince would practice between his legs, and occasionally lend to the princess, who enjoyed playing between her legs as well.

If Haydn hadn't written anything at all, he would still be famous as the man who taught both Mozart and Beethoven. Mozart learned how to form and structure, while Beethoven learned how to storm and fracture. Mozart's composition classes with Haydn really took off. Beethoven just took off.

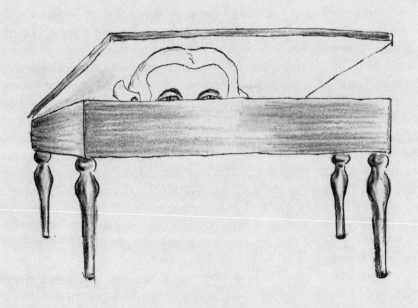

There is a famous story surrounding the *Farewell Symphony,* in which members of the orchestra finished their parts, blew out their candles and left the stage one by one while the symphony was still winding down. Haydn – who was already known as the father of the symphony and father of the string quartet – was now also known as the father of the Musician's Union. Nobody dared pooh-pooh Papa.

Haydn managed to write over 100 symphonies, 83 string quartets, 52 piano sonatas, concertos, and a great deal of chamber music. Also 23 operas, (including, of all things, a comic opera about space travel called *The World of the Moon!*) four oratorios and many songs and masses. Not bad for a peasant kid who used to saw his left arm with a stick, pretending it was a violin.

After his death, Joseph Haydn's skull was taken to be used by a medical student (it couldn't have been Berlioz – he was only six at the time) and kept changing hands until it landed in the lap of the Vienna Society of the Friends of Music. Even in death, Haydn was still showing the world how one gets a head in the social circles of Vienna.

Wolfgang Amadeus Mozart
b. Salzburg, Austria, 1756; d. Vienna, Austria, 1791

Mozart was the sort of person who could think up a string quartet in his head, and then write out the separate parts before committing the full score to paper. In other words, Wolfgang Amadeus Mozart was an alien.

When he and his sister Nannerl were little kids, their father Leopold paraded them all over Europe like a pair of trick dogs. The poor kids took turns becoming sick, which worried their father as he jotted down how much money they would lose that week.

After holding court in Vienna one day, six-year-old Wolfgang trundled away from the harpsichord and promptly slipped on the marble floor. It was none other than Marie Antoinette – only two months older – who helped him up. He was so grateful he offered to marry her. (Mozart loved older women.) She didn't exactly lose her head over him.

Leopold gleefully rubbed his avaricious hands together as Wolfgang performed blindfolded, or backwards, or spontaneously created a fugue based on a prince's impotent theme. The court was so bedazzled by this puffy-headed imp, some of the nobility were actually known to have severe identity crises after his visit. Leopold could have had a great retirement if he had known enough to start a royal psychiatric clinic.

There is a well-known story that occurred when Leopold brought his son to the Sistine Chapel. Allegri's *Miserere* was a sancrosanct *a cappella* choral work not heard outside the walls of the chapel. Nor could the sheet music be bought in the gift shop at the back. The 10-year-old Mozart listened to the glorious work intently, then later wrote the whole thing out from memory. (It would have been far more amazing if he had repainted the *ceiling* from memory.)

In 1772, Salzburg received a new Archbishop – Hieronymus von Colloredo. The Mozarts got off on the wrong foot with this vain man when Leopold asked permission to take his son on another concert tour. He was refused. Leopold didn't understand the expression "no way José" until he and Wolfgang were booted out of the Archbishop's service. Leopold was later reinstated but

Wolfgang took off for Germany, calling Hieronymus von Colloredo an "old prick."

He found his way to Mannheim and befriended many important artists. He also met the singer Fridolin Weber, who, fortunately, had several daughters. After a slightly more than musical liason with soprano Aloysia Weber, she dumped him, as she was looking to bag someone of greater importance. Mozart moved along the ranks to a younger sister, Constanze. His father was horrified with the choice of such a common girl but Mozart told him he loved her for her "two small black eyes and winsome figure" (big boobs).

It was a relatively happy marriage aside from the pressure of desperately trying to make a living. Mozart had become one of the first truly professional freelance musicians, and wrote good commercial music. His dress was always impeccable and of the finest materials. He had become accustomed to the 'look' his father had created for him. But his reputation was spotty and he didn't seem to care what he said about other musicians: "Like all Italians," Mozart once blathered, "Clementi is a charlatan ... he has not the slightest taste or expression." (I'm sure Salieri, as an Italian, didn't exactly extend an olive branch to Mozart – unless the olives were poisoned.) Meanwhile, Mozart was losing vast sums of money gambling and playing billiards – without telling Constanze.

He had written his first opera as a little kid and continued writing them now that he was a *big* kid. The only difference – his plots were getting worse. He wrote *The Impresario* and *The Marriage of Figaro* side by side, and may have mixed up some of the characters. (There's so much running in and out of these operas, no one would have noticed anyway.) Then he wrote *Don Giovanni* and *The Magic Flute*, in which one of the main characters is the precursor to Big Bird on *Sesame Street*.

All in all, Mozart's output was stunning. He wrote 41 symphonies; 25 piano concertos; 26 string quartets – I think I'll stop here because I'm having an identity crisis: By the time Mozart was my age, he was already three years dead. One composer with whom I empathize once said: "Mozart's music affects me so directly that it actually makes me feel sick." A French toast to Georges Bizet.

Ludwig van Beethoven
b. Bonn, Germany, 1770; d. Vienna, Austria, 1827

One of the great giants of Music Hystery was Ludwig van Beethoven, and he was only 5'4". One of his heroes was Napoleon (they could see eye to eye), for whom he dedicated his *Third Symphony*. Later, Beethoven had a bone to pick with Bonaparte after the latter declared himself Emperor. (I think our composer friend was just a wee bit jealous and wanted to conquer the world first.)

Beethoven met the young Mozart (he was never old) and astounded him with his improvisations. Wolfgang knew when he wasn't wanted and died shortly thereafter. Beethoven had to search out the second banana in Vienna, who was Haydn (and if he had known in advance the brusque personality this young composer possessed, he would have *remained* hidden). The 60-year-old Haydn tried in vain to teach all the rules Beethoven wanted to break. After Haydn finally broke off their relationship, Beethoven ensconced himself in the aristocratic circles of Vienna as a freelance pianist and composer. He broke many more rules – those of etiquette. Someone once talked during his performance and he stormed out of the drawing room screaming, "I will not play for such pigs!" He not only screamed at Prince Lobkowitz (who helped bring in his salary) but also lobbed eggs at a waiter (who helped bring in his celery) because the eggs were insufficiently fresh. At least he proved to be a humanist at heart: He yelled at the different classes of people with equanimity.

Beethoven became famous in Europe, but by the age of 29, he began losing the use of his most important organ (and he was also going deaf). His friend J.N. Mälzel, inventor of the metronome, made an ear-trumpet for Beethoven (not, by the way, a musical instrument to play by ear) but when the distraught composer tried listening through this device, all he could hear was the ticking of a damn metronome.

By the time his deafness began, Beethoven had already written two of his nine symphonies, so he had heard at least enough to get the other seven right. What he didn't need to hear was some of the criticism leveled at these works. After a Leipzig performance of his *Second Symphony*, a critic called it "a crude monstrosity, a serpent which continues to writhe about, refusing to die." Robert Schumann was kind to his *Fourth*, if not downright allegorical, calling it "a slender Grecian maiden between two Nordic giants." (Too bad Schumann's imagination didn't always make it into his own compositions.) Schumann's father-in-law, Friederich Wieck, wasn't so kind about one of Beethoven's other symphonies: "*The Seventh Symphony* could only have been written in a drunken state." (Since when did Beethoven visit Tennessee?) The majestic *Ninth Symphony* includes a choral movement at the end, praising Brotherhood, milk consumption, and other innumerable television commercials.

Development of his various movements were extensive – especially when it came to his bowels – but in his symphonies, the thematic ideas themselves are brief. For instance, the first movement of the famous *Fifth Symphony* is based on four notes – the 'Fate knocking on the door' theme. Beethoven never stayed in any place long enough to write more substantial themes, having moved over 40 times in Vienna alone. (No one helped him.) Coupled with the pounding of the piano and swearing till four in the morning, he did not exactly endear himself to his landlords. He was too deaf to tell if his playing had improved, but after having been kicked out of his apartment for the 39th time, his swearing had improved immensely.

To learn more about Beethoven, there are all kinds of movies one can rent. But don't be confused by a film called *Beethoven* – about a big lovable St. Bernard. This saint also happens to be the unofficial patron saint of composers, as long as there's a flask around his neck.

Gioacchino Rossini
b. Pesaro, Italy, 1792; d. Passy, France, 1868

'Ditty-bum ditty-bum ditty-bum bum bum ...'

Gioacchino Rossini is known as much for his television music as Richard Strauss is for his film music. Bugs Bunny and Lone Ranger fans will be surprised to learn that some of their favourite music was written by a chunky 19th-century composer turned chef. (*If music be the love of food, read on ...*)

Well-rounded a composer that he was, other composers considered him too much of a lightweight to understand serious art. "Give me the laundry bill and I will set it to music," he once said. (Those other composers may have been right.) One composer thought highly enough of Rossini to send him a score to look at. "I have just received a Stilton and a cantata from Cipriani Potter," Rossini told his friends. "The cheese was superb."

Rossini didn't take weighty Teutonic epic drama too seriously: "Mr. Wagner has beautiful moments, but bad quarters of an hour." On Tannhauser: "It is music one must hear several times. I'm not going again." (Just as a piece of conjecture, I imagine Rossini wouldn't have made it through one of Wagner's operas without starving to death – and he called *Bach* a "colossal creature."!!)

The premiere of his most famous opera – *The Barber of Seville* – was like an accident waiting to happen. The audience hissed and booed (unless they were yelling *'Bis! Bis!'* which is what Italians do when they want to hear it again – but I doubt it). The character Basilio fell down some stairs and a meowing cat wandered on stage. Rossini took off out the back door – presumably to write his famous cat duet.

Rossini married a leading soprano (what else?) by the name of Isabella, which began a long-winded, uncomical soap opera, a shame for the man who specialized in long-winded comical opera. (Just as another piece of conjecture: Could those long-winded – or should I say, florid, vertigo-inducing – arias be meant for his-a-bella wife, Isabella, as punishment?)

Singers of Rossini's time embellished arias so completely one would have been hard-pressed to recognize the composer.

Rossini once accompanied a young singer who embroidered her way around an aria from *The Barber of Seville*. When she finished he congratulated her on her lovely singing and asked who the composer was.

Another fashionable travesty in Rossini's mind was the audience's adulation for tenors and their loud, bleating high notes. Enrico Tamberlik was a singer of this persuasion who enraptured the hordes with his prolonged top C sharp. Tamberlik once visited Rossini at home. "Let him in," Rossini ordered. "But tell him to leave his C sharp on the coat rack. He can pick it up on the way out."

Asked his opinion as to who might be the greatest Italian composer, Rossini replied, "Mozart," which just goes to show he didn't pay attention in Music Hystery or geography class.

The penultimate anecdote is left to Rossini. Naturally, food is involved:

"The best time to compose an Overture," he once wrote, "is to wait until the evening before opening night. Nothing primes inspiration more than necessity, whether it be the presence of a copyist waiting for your work or the prodding of an impresario tearing his hair. In my time, all the impresarios in Italy were bald at thirty. ... I composed the overture to *Otello* in a little room in the Barbaja palace wherein the baldest and fiercest of directors had forcibly locked me with a lone plate of spaghetti and the threat that I would not be allowed to leave the room alive until I had written the last note."

By the age of 38, after having written 38 operas, he gave up composing altogether to lead the good life. He realized instead of a good *recitativo secco* he'd rather enjoy a good *vino secco*. The writing must have been on the wall because Rossini reached a point when he was too lazy to climb out of bed to write down his ideas. This may have been the origin of the term 'sheet music.'

Franz Schubert
b. Vienna, Austria, 1797; d. Vienna, Austria, 1828

Franz Schubert, that germane leader of German lieder, began his musical career as a choirboy in the Court Chapel of Vienna. Aware of the importance of posterity and puberty, the chunky little chorister wrote in one of the scores of a mass: 'Schubert, Franz, crowed for the last time 26 July, 1812.' (A good year for making overtures.)

Schubert's nickname was 'Tubby' and he was only 5'1". (No wonder he looked up to Beethoven). He must have known he was going to die young, for he wrote 140 songs in 1815. But then he slacked off in 1816, and only wrote 100. Of course that year he also wrote a *Stabat Mater*, two cantatas, two symphonies, chamber music and an opera. Isn't it amazing what one can accomplish when *The Simpsons* aren't on every day.

One of his friend's brothers loved his songs so much, Schubert felt compelled to copy one out for him – from memory – after having consumed two bottles of wine. The song happened to be *The Trout*. The wine must have been white since it goes best with fish.

Every once in a while, an evening of Schubert's music was performed in a fashionable salon,with the composer himself at the keyboard, flanked by a dozen or two adoring fans. These musical events became known as Schubertiads, where punch was drunk and Schubert became punch drunk. If he didn't possess a swelled head on those evenings, he certainly did the next morning.

Schubert always travelled in interesting Viennese circles. He became an important member of the *Gesellschaft der Musikfreunde*, where he rubbed elbows with some of the capital's finest musicians (including Czerny, who no doubt performed the latest in finger exercises). He also became an important member of many other Viennese establishments, where he did much more than just rub elbows and exercise fingers. It was at this point he contracted syphilis. (See Phyllis.)

Musically speaking, Schubert's best-known hooker was *Gretchen at the Spinning-Wheel*. While recovering from a bad bout of syphilis in hospital, he wrote the song cycle *Die Schöne*

Müllerin. Needless to say, these songs became highly infectious.

A respected Austrian lawyer (how times change!) blamed Schubert's debauched lifestyle on his friend and roommate Franz Schober (whom Schubert jokingly called Franz Schobert). Many derogatory comments were made against this *scheiss* disturber and how his bad influence left Schubert "bathed in slime." It was Schober who brought out the hedonism and ill-behaved manner in the young composer. He also brought out the opium. One cannot blame Schubert's friends entirely on his behaviour: Mental illness does occasionally run in certain families – and with the Schubert's, it positively galloped.

His swan songs – 17 of them – were aptly named *Schwanen- gesang*. Schubert, Franz, crowed for the very last time 19th November, 1828. He is best known for the works he didn't finish.

Hector Berlioz
b. La Cote-St André, France, 1803; d. Paris, France, 1869

Hector Berlioz's *Memoirs* is one of the greatest achievements of the Romantic era, and is more beautifully embellished than a Rococo bathtub. His parents lived in a rural village surrounded by a hectare of barley-oats, so they had no trouble naming their only son. The father was a country doctor who apparently was the first to bring the ancient art of acupuncture to France. Naturally, M. Berlioz constantly needled young Hector into becoming a doctor. The son hadn't the gall or liver to object, nor the heart to refuse his dad's cash, so he went off to Paris and entered into the field of medicine.

Berlioz bided his time in the dissection room singing arias to himself as he sawed skulls in half. He wondered constantly how he could make the leap to music from cutting people up. Music criticism is similar, but that didn't occur to him until later.

To his parent's dismay, Berlioz left medicine and entered the Paris *Conservatoire* – but by the wrong door (the one only women could use). The head of the *Conservatoire*, the composer Luigi Cherubini, chased him out, cursing in Italian – the proper language in music education. This was but a microcosm of musical politics that plagued Berlioz for the rest of his life.

As the years went by, Berlioz took revenge on all the meddling, unjust Cherubinis of France by immortalizing anything that wasn't French – including Shakespeare, Goethe's *Faust, Benvenuto Cellini, Harold in Italy*, the *Hungarian March*, etc. As a result, every country loved him but his own.

The other non-French object he immortalized was the Irish actress Harriet Smithson. She was translated into a tune about 40 bars long (known as the *idée fixe* – she became a 'fixed idea' in poor Berlioz's smitten little brain.) This tune appears under many guises in his humbly titled *Symphonie Fantastique* – one of the greatest opium-induced masterpieces in Music Hystery.

After losing out the first couple of years, Berlioz finally won the *Prix de Rome* and the Revolution of 1830 broke out shortly after. He went off to Italy but first became engaged to Camille Moke, a young, attractive pianist who enjoyed playing for men as long as the instrument was upright.

While in Rome, Berlioz became fast friends with Mendelssohn and was amazed with his fluency at the keyboard (Berlioz never learned the piano). Mendelssohn was impressed with Berlioz's hair, but later wrote that Berlioz "had not a spark of talent" and that his instruments "vomited music as though they had a hangover." Some friend.

While in Italy, Berlioz received a letter from Camille Moke's mother saying the engagement was off and Camille was seeing a man who manufactured pianos. Berlioz, jealous of Gesualdo's place in Music Hystery as the only murdering composer, decided to correct this wrong by plotting to murder his fiancée, her lover and her mother (for sending such a miserable letter). He hired seamstresses to make women's clothing so he could kill his victims incognito – or, at the very least, kill them in style. Berlioz boarded a coach for Paris, but aborted the mission about halfway there. He didn't want his *Memoirs* to end with a deceptive cadence.

Berlioz later married Harriet Smithson, but as her star began to fade her drinking began to shine, and he suddenly realized that his Shakespearean esthetic was becoming more of a spurious ascetic.

Berlioz attended orchestral performances and ranted aloud when certain instruments failed to appear, due to budget cuts. In 1833, he became music critic for *Journal des débats* so he could rant professionally. This he did for 30 years – in very LARGE print, for his criticisms were as loud as his music.

Rather than unleashing his voice inside the concert hall and going hoarse, Berlioz unleashed a horse in the concert hall with voices inside. *Les Troyens* – complete with Trojan horse – was a spectacular flop in 1863, but has since been remounted successfully in many cities, with or without walls.

Another disaster as far as the audience was concerned was *La Damnation de Faust*. Faust is dragged down to Hell on horseback before the curtain closes. A similar incident happened just after the curtain closed on Berlioz's life: As his body was nearing the cemetery, drawn by horses, they reared and galloped toward the gates. The mourners were aghast at the sight of the hearse out of control, but the horses slowed and calmly trotted onto the sacred ground – perhaps amused with themselves for having given their apoplectic audience a typical Berliozian *adieu*.

Johann Strauss
b. Vienna, Austria, 1825: d. Vienna, Austria, 1899

This Viennese violinist/composer/conductor was said to have 'champagne flowing through his veins,' which explains why he conducted as though he had a cork up his butt. In fact, he himself, the Waltz-King, admitted he couldn't dance to save his wife – of which there were three, and only one witch.

His father, Johann Strauss Sr., had been Europe's king of dance music for much too long, and conveniently died just in time to pass the baton to his son. Strauss the younger inherited from his dad four 'Strauss orchestras,' but his house wasn't big enough to store them all. He realized he was going to have to work like a dog to keep all these instrumentalists employed. So he rented a coach and raced all over Vienna (fortunately the city is designed so that it is easy to go in circles), barely making it in time for the next gig.

All of Vienna came to love him – especially women and doctors, because Johann Strauss was considered good-looking, and a wealthy hypochondriac. This mass adulation sometimes got Strauss into trouble. A Russian officer was most apologetic when he had to challenge the composer to a duel. His wife had been sending Strauss roses every day and it was becoming a thorny issue for the young Russki. Strauss took him back to his villa and showed him two entire rooms filled with flowers, and hundreds of love letters. The officer put his pistols away and left the villa – damning himself for having entered the wrong vocation.

Being engaged 13 times to young starry-eyed hopefuls probably drove Strauss batty – appropriate for the composer whose masterpiece was an operetta called *Die Fledermaus* – but he finally settled down with Henriette Jetty, a singer. She already had five children with other men, and Strauss didn't know some of these children existed until a deadbeat showed up at the door looking for his 'mother.' He demanded money from both of them and was briskly waltzed out of the house by an indignant Strauss. Henriette died shortly after this ordeal. Wife number two was a total disaster. Angelika Dittrich was a (cough) singer – 25 years younger than Strauss. Vienna, being Vienna, loves its schnitzel,

dark beer and gossip. It can talk Ringstrasses around other cities when it comes to gossip, and now the place was rife with it. Angelika was reveling in affairs just as Strauss came up with a real flop called *Blind Cow*. (Strauss was never any good at choosing subject matter – or wives, for that matter.) His third and last wife, Adele, was the most faithful of the lot, and was secretly called 'Cosima in three-four time' – alluding to Wagner's devoted wife.

An invitation came from Boston to conduct just over 14 concerts. The fee: $100,000 – and I don't mean Canadian dollars! As it turned out, that's also how many people came to just one concert. The Americans were so Strauss-crazy, gaggles of women were demanding locks of his hair. One of his entourage made everyone happy by selling them generous strands of thick black hair – from the back of a Newfoundland dog. (A great irony if the dog had been an offspring of Wagner's Newfoundlander.)

Strauss became fabulously wealthy after *The Blue Danube* was published. It has been popular from 1867 to *2001* and put not only the publisher Spina on the map, but also Stanley Kubrick.

Curiously, the American author Mark Twain crops up twice in this book. He happened to be Strauss's last visitor before he died, and also turns up as a friend of the wife of Charles Ives. And ne'er the Twain shall meet two more disparate composers.

The Grim Reaper danced Strauss off the ballroom floor in his 74th year, and an outdoor concert was interrupted mid-stream so that the *Blue Danube* could be played. The Viennese realized what had happened and collectively cried a river.

Most of his waltzes have been well preserved – just like his body, with all that champagne flowing through it.

Felix Mendelssohn
b. Hamburg, Germany, 1809; d, Leipzig, Germany, 1847

Felix Mendelssohn wasn't exactly your typical starving artist. When he was a mere 13 years old, his father hired a chamber orchestra so the boy could conduct his own compositions. For those who are weak of stomach or high of blood pressure, I suggest you stop reading here.

Mendelssohn was a cute little kid who had been the muse of the elderly Goethe, the darling of musical circles throughout Europe, friend of most great composers, marriage bait for all eligible women, and occasional vocal instructor for Queen Victoria! How the Dickens does one get into a family like his? (Oh yes, he met Dickens too.)

This was one boy who could do very little wrong in the eyes of his father Abraham, a millionaire banker. Felix was a prodigy at the keyboard, and so was his sister Fanny. The siblings travelled and performed extensively together (à la Wolfgang and Nannerl) and became so close that friends in later years jokingly suggested they marry. When Felix handed Fanny new compositions for her approval, she would cough after noticing something she didn't like; when she handed Felix new compositions for *his* approval, he would derive great pleasure from patting his bright little Fanny.

He loved his Fanny so much, he started writing his famous piano pieces – *Songs Without Words* – which were dedicated to her. By the time Mendelssohn was through there were 48 of them. (That's an awful lot of music in which nothing is said.)

Abraham bought a house in Leipzig for his family, which was so large, the servants in the East wing spoke a different German dialect from those in the West wing. But money isn't everything, and Mendelssohn had to work just as hard as the next privileged, handsome, millionaire composer in Music Hystery – except there wasn't a next one. Mendelssohn was crest-fallen when one of his obscure operas (they were all obscure) was critiqued by the newspaper as being "not bad for a rich man's son."

He left his own compositions for awhile (he didn't take kindly to criticism) and concentrated on an extremely noble project. J. S. Bach's music was very difficult to find in the 19th

century. He was regarded as a rusty old antique who should be left in his grave – much like the Titanic. But the 20-year-old Mendelssohn had an invested interest in the *St. Matthew Passion*, both as a Jew *and* a Lutheran, and single-handedly resurrected Christ and Bach at the same time. He astonished the old curmudgeons at the *Singakademie* when a few hundred enthusiastic musicians crawled out of the woodwork, and performed the *Passion* to an ebullient packed house – a stone's throw from where Bach had once lived and worked and made babies. What Music Hystery has always neglected to tell us is that both audience and performers were Bach's descendants.

Mendelssohn travelled to Scotland and was so inspired by the grandeur of Fingal's Cave, he wrote the *Hebrides Overture* – better known as *Fingal's Cave*. It was the perfect location for the venturing Romantic soul: The cave itself drinks in the pounding waves of the sea and looks like the doorway of a large temple. The overture captures the swelling water so effectively, the orchestra members usually leave the stage soaking wet.

Mendelssohn completed his oratorio *St. Paul* in 1836 and there were mixed reviews. George Bernard Shaw said he would "sooner talk Sunday school for two hours and a half to a beautiful woman with no brains as listen to *St. Paul* over again." And that is when Mendelssohn got married.

He married Cécile Jeanrenaud, a pretty yet pretty empty-headed girl who made Fanny pretty jealous. Unfortunately, the *Wedding March* from *A Midsummer Night's Dream* was not played during the marriage because Felix hadn't written it yet. (They probably had to make do with that 'Here comes the bride – short, fat and wide' tune of Wagner's.)

A Midsummer Night's Dream was written in 1843. Artists and critics alike have given full marks to this incidental music as the most Shakespearean ever – Bard none. It was now Fanny's turn to congratulate Felix over his splendid Bottom.

Mendelssohn's other masterpieces are unquestionably the *Violin Concerto in E minor*, and his oratorio *Elijah*. For any disputation, there *is* a toll-free number: 1-800-LEIPZIG.

Fanny died in 1847 – a real bummer for Felix. He had told her he would join her for her next birthday – which he did, and died barely six months later.

Robert Schumann
b. Zwickau, Germany, 1810; d. Endenich, Germany, 1856

Finally, a father in Music Hystery who didn't want his budding little composer to be a lawyer – it was the mother this time. Mr. Schumann had long been – dare I say it? – decomposing.

The scales of justice were once again outweighed by the scales of the piano. Schumann studied with Friederich Wieck, the best-known teacher in Leipzig. Robert became impatient as to his progress and devised a contraption that held one finger immobile while the adjacent finger exercised. Schumann could have patented this as the first digital gadget in the music business, but sadly, his third finger became paralyzed. He had now given the music world his middle finger and had to think of another way to prostitu – ah, offer his services to his chosen field. Then it dawned on him – those who can't do, criticize.

Schumann started the *Neue Zeitschrift für Musik* (New Musical Review) and attacked composers and performers with equal enthusiastic zeal. Of Carl Czerny he wrote: "If I had enemies and wanted to destroy them, I would condemn them to listen to nothing but music like this ..." (Mind you, he may have been a little jealous of Czerny, since it was he who created all those finger exercises that Schumann could no longer play.)

Friederich Wieck had a 13-year-old daughter with big eyes who was already God's gift to perfection at the keyboard. Wieck had seen to that. Clara was a fetching girl and the idea of marrying such a young thing within eight years must have seemed far-fetched to Schumann. Wieck was insanely possessive of Clara and made ludicrous accusations against Robert – his own student – to mar his reputation. He even went so far as to endorse one of Clara's rivals – Camille Pleyel – the pianist who seems to pop up in nearly every Romantic composer's biography (including Berlioz's, in which she was nearly popped off). In 1840, Robert and Clara married and Mendelssohn performed at the wedding. He hadn't written his wedding march yet so he was forced to sing instead. Marrying Clara had made Robert so happy he decided to postpone his suicide. His father-in-law, Wieck, was sent to prison for a couple of weeks because he had called Schumann an alcoholic. Schumann celebrated with two bottles of his favourite brandy.

Robert and Clara moved to Dresden in 1844, then Düsseldorf in 1850. *Poco a poco,* Schumann began to suffer from manic depression – or 'severe melancholia,' just to give it more of a Romantic *stürm und drang* flavour. But this deterioration did not deter the ration of children he and Clara were having. He had created 248 songs and eight children – one child for every 31 songs.

The ninth child to appear on their doorstep was Brahms, who had brought along his own sleeping bag and toothbrush. Clara had been championing Schumann's lugubrious piano works and now began interpreting the lugubrious piano works of Brahms. This young composer became a lifelong friend of the Schumanns and it has to be said that his eyes became a little too big for his britches while looking upon Clara. It also has to be said that Brahms' britches became a little too big for Clara's eyes, as he became one of the fattest composers in living memory.

One day, Schumann went off for a leisurely stroll and threw himself into the Rhine. When a pair of boatmen recognized Schumann as a composer, they flipped a coin to see if they should save him or not. (They did, and I imagine Brahms had unkind thoughts about them from that point on. Well, they were only vulgar boatmen). Schumann died in an asylum at Endenich, and to Brahms's credit, he kept his hands off Clara until she died 40 years later. (Just to Clara-fy – Brahms kept his hands off Clara after she died, too.)

Schumann was responsible for four symphonies and a lot of piano music. Perhaps too much piano music.

Franz Liszt
b. Raiding, Hungary, 1811; d. Bayreuth, Germany, 1886

"Liszt's soul is too tender, too artistic, too impressionable, for him to live without the company of women. He must have a number of them around him, just as in his orchestra he needs many instruments, with various rich timbres." If this florid piece of descriptive tripe – conceived, no less, by a princess – had been written today, it would have been postulated with more of a prosaic vernacular, thus: "Liszt wants lotsa sex."

And what Liszt wanted, Liszt got. He had affairs by the scores (scores that were well orchestrated) – mostly with aristocratic and fashionable women, which accounted for the many countesses. The most celebrated opus in his catalogue was the Countess Marie D'Agoult, whose pseudonym was Daniel Stern – no relation to the villain from *Home Alone I* or *II*. He even went after the brilliant young pianist Camille Pleyel, the girl who had disengaged herself from Berlioz and was nearly murdered as a result. When Liszt met up with her she was married to Ignaz Pleyel, the famous piano manufacturer. Presumably, Liszt wanted to keep a lid on it. Neither did he want to put a damper on the marriage, nor have any strings attached.

Liszt was one of the greatest virtuosos of any era and admired his homely profile so much he decided to inflict it upon the audience. On stage, he turned the piano so that the adoring masses could view the pianist from the side as opposed to the backside. Surely, this was so that Liszt could keep abreast of the audience as well. Indeed, one woman went so far as to place Liszt's butt between her bosom. He had tossed away the tail end of his cigar, which she had endeavoured to retrieve and then sewed it into her corsage. It remained there for more than a quarter of a century.

The narcissistic pianist/composer used the Catholic religion as an excuse to back away from the fair sex, when it was convenient for him. He decided to become an Abbé and dressed in a long black cassock. This must have made a stark contrast with his long and flowing silver hair. (Salivating women were actually known to have plucked these hairs from his head as he

was playing – a form of *pizzicato* this musician could have done without.)

In 1861, one of Liszt's students – supposedly a young Englishman – threw himself at the aging pianist. He turned out to be a woman in drag, which was a disguise to escape a jealous husband. In musical affairs this is known as an 'enharmonic change,' tending toward the flat side of the scale.

Finally it happened. Liszt met up with a madwoman by the name of Olga Janina, a student, an aristocrat, and a Cossack all rolled up into one explosive package. It was a case of the Cossack vs. the cassock. She unfurled her pointed Eastern European tongue and coolly exclaimed: "He shall be mine, or I will kill him." It nearly came to be. One impassioned evening, as the two were tightly embracing, a poised, poisoned dagger awaited his next words to her. If they were of love, she would spare him; if they were not, she would pare him. She waited with bated – or is that baited?– breath, but fate abated, and hence they mated. (Now, wasn't that nicely understated?)

Liszt was best known for his piano transcriptions, which made him ooodles of money.

Frédéric Chopin
b. Zelazowa Wola, Poland, 1810; d. Paris, France, 1849

His father was a bookkeeper, which could explain why there are so many ledger lines in Chopin's piano music. He collaborated with his youngest sister in writing a one-act comedy *The Mistake*. Needless to say, he never collaborated with his youngest sister again.

In 1825, Chopin improvised upon one of the instruments invented about that time which aimed to unite the harmonium with the pianoforte. The result was the pianomonium – often mistaken for pandemonium.

In 1829, he fell in love with a student at the Warsaw Conservatory – Constantia Gladowska, yet another young nut-brown-haired soprano who has unwittingly made it into the annals of Music Hystery. And another smitten composer bites the dust.

Chopin was one of the most astonishing pianists ever, but because of his chronic poor health, he was usually too feeble to lift his foot from the pedal, resulting in a trend of "dreamy poignancy." This revolutionized the whole approach to pianistic technique and proves that if one is to start a new musical style at the keyboard, one must simply put one's foot down.

The *Revolutionary Étude* is not a study of war, but a rip-roaring piano work that illustrates Chopin's anguished condition when Russia took Warsaw in 1831. Of course, this work has to be performed with a great deal of Polish.

He met Robert Schumann in 1835 – a composer of great literacy and taste. Schumann wrote of Chopin in one of his articles, "Hats off gentlemen, a genius!" A certain gentlemen who gave the biggest tip of the hat in Chopin's direction was George Sand. "I have met a great celebrity, Mme. Dudevant, known as George Sand," Chopin wrote. "Her appearance is not to my liking. Indeed there is something about her which positively repels me ... What an unattractive person La Sand is ... Is she really a woman? I'm inclined to doubt it."

George Sand, otherwise known as Aurore Dudevant, was a novelist who wore tailored suits and smoked huge cigars. She would weep under the piano while Chopin played his delicate

works. This was Chopin's healthiest relationship – discounting the second-hand smoke.

As do most great composers, Chopin eventually died – but not before having said: "The three most celebrated doctors on the island have been to see me. One sniffed at what I spat, the second tapped where I spat from, and the third sounded me and listened as I spat. The first said I was dead, the second that I was dying, and the third that I'm going to die."

Giuseppe Verdi
b. Le Roncole, Italy, 1813; d. Milan, Italy, 1901

Giuseppe Verdi (otherwise known as Joe Green) is undoubtedly the most famous operatic composer who ever lived. His parents were tavern keepers, so it was apparent that when it came to writing 'Brindisi' songs – or songs with alcoholic content – it ran in Giuseppe's blood.

When Verdi was just an infant, the Austrian and Russian armies were rooting the French out of northern Italy, and were indiscriminately massacring everyone in their path. Mrs. Verdi took her baby up into the belfry of a church and saved both their lives as the carnage intensified below.

As an altar boy, Giuseppe was entranced by the sound of the organ and would go off into a sort of pipe dream, until one day he forgot to carry out his altar duties. The priest elbowed him and sent him flying down the chancel steps. (The Austrians and Russians couldn't shoot the boy in church, but the priest gave him his best shot.) Verdi was embarrassed by the fall. He turned to the priest and said: "OH pa-ter, OH pa-ter ..." which became the inspiration for the rhythm in many of his solos and choruses – especially 'Brindisi' songs.

Verdi played pianoforte duets with the nubile daughter of the noble merchant Antonio Barezzi. It seemed to Barezzi that Margherita and Giuseppe had chosen quite a number of duets that required innumerable far-reaching hand-crossings. The result was the inevitable tying-up of knots. They tied the knot on May 4th,1836.

Like so many composers, tragedy struck. Death stole away his infant son, daughter, and the lovely Margherita just as he was commissioned to write a comic opera. The opera, *Un giorno di regno*, died a quicker death than any of his family.

In 1842, he penned the opera *Nabucodonosor,* which everyone calls *Nabucco* because they couldn't fit the whole name on the marquee. Its great success at La Scala was due in part to the excellent singers. The soprano Giuseppina Strepponi acquitted herself famously (and later on was infamously acquitted). She had had two illegitimate children before meeting up with Verdi, and their union became more than just musical.

This scandalized the town of Busetto, his near birthplace, and it took 10 years for their 'marriage' to become legitimate. (Why is it never a contralto?)

Over the years, Verdi wrote the operas *Rigoletto, Il Trovatore*, and *La Traviata* and was equalled by no one save Mozart in the delineation of character and melodic invention. (Although, as far as plots go, no one could save Mozart: He was more interested in defamation of character and moronic intention.)

In 1870, Verdi was commissioned to write an opera for the opening of the Suez Canal. *Aïda* was elephantine in its success – mostly because of the parading elephants. Those opera companies that can't afford elephants usually have to settle for the truncated version.

Those many years before, when Verdi, in a fit of depression, threw the libretto of *Nabucco* onto the table, it opened to the words: *'Va, pensiero, sull' ali dorate.'* ('Go thought, on golden wings.') The writing was filled with such contemporary meaning, due to the suffering of Jews in captivity, Verdi knew that the opera had to be written. Many years later, this 'peasant chorus' would move Verdi in a different way: 28,000 people lined the streets and spontaneously started humming *Va, pensiero* as a horse-drawn hearse carried the great composer to his final resting place. As a tribute to the underlying meaning of the text, they had the horse circumcised.

Richard Wagner
b. Leipzig, Germany, 1813; d. Venice, Austria, 1883

There have been as many books written about him as Napoleon, Hitler and Christ. Hitler even named his autobiography *Mein Kampf* as a sort of tribute to this composer's autobiography, *My Life*. The little Nazi empathized with the anti-Semitic enthusiasms of Wagner and particularly enjoyed hearing the phallic *leitmotif* of Siegfried's sword as his strapping Aryan troops went goosestepping by.

Richard Wagner wasn't sure who his father was. He was either a policeman named Friederich (his mother's husband) or a painter/actor/poet named Ludwig (*not* his mother's husband – until later). Richard the boy was shipped off to grammar school in Dresden and was a horrendous student unless he was reading Greek literature. In 1826 his entire family moved to Leipzig. Richard, desperate to be with them, lied to the headmaster and went off on his own little odyssey until he arrived home(r).

Wagner decided to become a composer and wrote *Overture in B flat*. He thought of the different sections of the orchestra as colours: The themes of the winds, green; the strings, red; and the brass black. The audience must have known that the result of green, red and black when mixed is brown – they called the overture an odious substance representative of that particular colour.

In 1836, Richard married an aspiring, flighty actress named Minna Planer. The day after their marriage, Wagner was summoned before the magistrate because he was indebted to so many people without very much intent of paying them back – a recurring *leitmotif* in his life. Just as Gesualdo's music (three centuries previous) had become more chromatic as he was hiding from his demons, so too did Wagner's music as he was hiding from his creditors. (It's ironic he should own a Newfoundland dog named Robber.) He had to abide loathsome musical transcription jobs from publishers, during which time he laboured stave after stave to stave off starvation.

Then it happened. His opera *Rienzi* was an unmitigated overnight success – in other words, everyone forgot about it the next day. But the name Wagner was about to become a

haus-hold name throughout Germany and the world. Operas such as The *Flying Dutchman, Tristan and Isolde, Tannhäuser*, and *Lohengrin* flowed from his pen.

A great story comes from a performance of *Lohengrin*. The charismatic, gregarious bass Leo Slezak was all set to climb aboard the prop swan, when an overzealous stage hand pulled its rope too early. As the disheartened singer watched the prop roll across the stage, he whispered during a rest: "What time does the next swan leave?"

One of *Lohengrin*'s biggest fans and a Wagner fanatic was King Ludwig – the mad king of Bavaria. Not only did he pay off the composer's enormous debts, he stuck him in a palatial home with servants and gave him a salary that made local politicians freak. After writing *Tristan and Isolde* and *The Mastersingers*, Wagner embarked on a project so large, it went on to immortalize horns and breastplates, intermissions, and *Apocalypse Now*. Of course I'm referring to *The Ring Cycle* – lovingly known to the unwashed as *The Rinse Cycle*.

Wagner was much better at conducting musical affairs than personal affairs: He had stolen, yet again, a woman from a friend. The conductor Hans von Bülow so admired Wagner, he felt privileged handing his wife Cosima over to him. Another friend, Liszt, wasn't so enamoured with this marital hopscotch – Cosima was his daughter. Wagner couldn't bear children, so Cosima bore him two, and named them Siegfried and Isolde.

Thanks to the Mad King's obsession with Wagner, the composer was able to see his idea of *Gesamkunstwerk* (all art coming together) come together. Wagner had designed a theatre in the small town of Bayreuth that would properly accommodate his creations, but not enough fundraising was to be had. It was King Ludwig who put in enough florins to put enough floor in. Even today, opera-lovers will fly seven hours to Bayreuth so they can hear 18 hours of chubby women singing through 47 keys. If you are planning a Wagnerian holiday, just remember to tell your travel agent it's *Bayreuth* – not Beirut.

Charles Gounod
b. Paris, France, 1818; d. St. Cloud, France, 1893

Gounod once said "the revelation of German music to me is like a bomb falling on a house and could cause me serious damage." All Gounod had to do was wait until the next century to see his prophecy come true. Eventually, Gounod dropped one of his own bombs on a couple of houses, which caused *him* serious damage: His opera *Sappho* briefly played in France and England, then crashed and burned.

There must exist a small Liszt of composers who wanted to become priests. Gounod himself entered a Carmelite seminary until he realized that this cloistered lifestyle was not conducive to putting grand operatic works on the stage. That is, not until Francis Poulenc showed up in the wings. (Poulenc wrote *Dialogue of the Carmelites*.)

Gounod was told by a Madame Zimmerman that he should either marry her daughter Anna, or simply stay away from her. He arrived at their door with a letter proclaiming that he was just a poor composer and had better decline. Madame Zimmerman excitedly whisked him into the house, and without noticing his letter, celebrated her daughter's impending marriage. Gounod was too polite to disobey this battle-ax of a woman and married Anna. Could this have prompted his writing of *Faust*?

Not only did Gounod become a husband in spite of himself, but he also became a recognized composer in spite of the bombing of *Sappho*, and another deadly opera, *Ulysse*. He had written a little *Ave Maria,* which became number one on the Parisian pop charts. It made so much money Gounod had to stop complaining about its gargantuan success.

Faust, his major opera, surprisingly didn't attract as many people as one would have thought. At least when a Wagner opera opened in Paris there were enough rows of people to start a riot. Gounod's operas had only enough people to start a row.

With *Faust*, Gounod was bought outright so that all proceeds of the opera sold in France and Belgium went to the greedy little publishers. Come to think of it, Gounod should have thought about Faust's soul before signing his score away.

Gounod moved to London in 1870 and met up with the

soprano Georgina Weldon. She was an insufferable suffragette who became a leading advocate for the change of lunacy laws in England. (She took up this cause once she discovered that her husband Harry was going to have her committed.) In spite of her husband, she was committed to Gounod for the longest time, calling him "my chicken" as he called her "my mousie." (She couldn't have changed the lunacy laws very drastically).

In 1872, Georgina and Gounod entered a little skirmish with Novello, his publishing company, which, in its own embarrassment, was responsible for sending one of the world's most famous composers to jail. Gounod enjoyed prison, as he could concentrate peacefully on his compositions. He swore like a trouper when he found out his mother-in-law paid to set him free. *C'est la vie.*

Jacques Offenbach
b. Cologne, Germany, 1819; d. Paris, France, 1880

If anybody could write a can-can, Offenbach could-could.

He was accepted into the Paris *Conservatoire* when he was only 14 by the same fellow who had made Berlioz's life hell – Luigi Cherubini. He was so put off by this Italian's music textbook, he doodled in the margins. (What's the matter with that? That's how *I* got started!)

Offenbach's works actually got off to a slow start because he was continually being thwarted by *l'Opera-Comique* – essentially the only house suitable for his light frothy works. Knowing his countrymen were among the best snubbers in the world (as in the perennial plights and perils of a certain Monsieur Berlioz), Offenbach kicked up his heels and opened his own 50-seat theatre, naming it *Theatre des Bouffes-Parisiens*. This does not mean 'theatre of the naked Parisians,' although it *was* meant to expose whatever Offenbach cared to show off.

Bouffes-Parisiens became famous for its catchy tunes and the reviews of its Revues were favourable. Offenbach became a Parisian poster-*garçon* and threw memorable parties. It was at one of these gatherings that Bizet showed up in diapers, Gustave Doré walked on his hands – etching this event in the minds of all those present – and the composer Delibes demonstrated how realistically he could bark like a dog. Such was the milieu of the Parisian elite.

It was the work *Orphee aux Enfers* that skyrocketed Offenbach to fame, landing him safely on a plateau from which he could attack the dreaded Richard Wagner – whom the French were already satirizing by rote, and satirizing Bayreuth.

The Tales of Hoffman was Offenbach's most famous operetta, but it is connected to a tale of tragedy: The second night it was performed in Vienna, a major fire broke out and many Wieners were roasted. After this disaster, his operettas did not come bach offen.

I leave the last word to Wagner: "Offenbach's music is a dung-heap upon which all the swine in Europe wallow." No wonder Offenbach didn't care much for Wagner's music.

Bedrich Smetana
b. Litomysl, Czechslovakia, 1824;
d. Prague, Czechslovakia, 1884

Bedrich's mom had a dream. An angel appeared to her and said that her unborn child would be a boy and would become a great musician. Bedrich's dad had a dream too. The devil appeared to him and said that his unborn child would be a boy and would become a great lawyer. The angel won out, and the great musician went on to lead one of the most harrowing lives in Music Hystery and eventually died in an insane asylum. Race to the bar, anyone?

Like most great musicians, Smetana found that school was getting in the way, and quit by the age of 16. His father gently (or maybe not so gently) suggested that perhaps he should lead a more pastoral life shoveling cow dung on the family farm – a more stable lifestyle, so to speak. When Smetana declined, his father became hopping mad – a natural reaction for someone who managed a brewery.

Smetana went to Plzen (when Czechoslovakia split up, the Slovaks ran away with all the vowels) and fell in love with a cousin, Luise, for whom he wrote a polka. After having fallen in love with many subsequent girls, and having written many concurrent polkas, he fell in love with Katerina 'The Wild One' Kolarova, a pianist.

By 24, Smetana nearly committed suicide – the inordinate number of girls and polkas were finally taking their toll – but Franz Liszt stepped in and lent him enough money to start a music academy. Smetana married Kolarova and started replacing polkas with daughters. Unbelievably, three of his girls died in quick succession and the grieving composer wrote his *Piano Trio in G minor* to alleviate his sadness. The critics vehemently derided the work. The newspapers should have bounced these Czechs from their jobs, but Smetana bounced back himself and took his wife and remaining daughter to Göteborg, Sweden – a land where there *is* no shortage of vowels, especially the funny-looking ones. This new country loved Smetana – who, with his constant wanderlusting eye, thought the Swedes sweeter than Czech chicks.

Tragedy struck again. On the way back to Prague, Katerina died. Smetana pulled through by letting himself become attracted to Bettina – the 19-year-old sister of his brother's wife. Smetana probably realized she had to be the last because thematic material for a good polka was becoming more elusive. He taught her chess and occasionally let her win – he always enjoyed a good Czech-mate.

At this point, mentioning his most famous opera, *The Bartered Bride,* is perhaps appropriate. Slavishly Slavonic in style, the salivating, sardonic nay-sayers slandered Smetana. He paid them no heed, and decided to write *Má vlast* (*My Country*). He couldn't hear a thing when he immersed himself in *The Moldau* – the river that runs through Prague, and one of the more famous movements.

Smetana went quite mad (of course, trying to lip-read the Czech language would be enough to drive anyone around the bend) and when his doctors appeared, he attacked them violently, thinking they were music critics. He began imagining himself as Liszt or Wagner – even the emperor, with or without the clothes.

Bedrich became bedridden in the city's asylum. In the streets below, an organ grinder was playing a tune from *The Bartered Bride* as the sad, sorry life of that opera's creator came to a grinding halt.

Johannes Brahms

b. Hamburg, Germany, 1833; d. Vienna, Austria, 1897

Mahler once said: "I have gone all through Brahms now. All I can say of him is that he's a puny little dwarf with a rather narrow chest." Mahler was obviously speaking figuratively, for Brahms was anything but puny. As a teenager, Johannes started developing his gut feelings as to what direction his music would take. He also started developing his gut. He was paid two thalers and all the beer he could drink to play piano in the various taverns and brothels on Hamburg's waterfront.

In 1848, Brahms was strongly influenced by a performance of Joachim, the famous violinist. Some years later they became good friends and Joachim recommended him to Liszt and Schumann. In Weimar, Liszt generously played one of his new works for Brahms, and at the end, turned to find him fast asleep.

When Brahms woke up he was at the Schumanns' in Dresden. Embarrassed by his sudden appearance, he felt compelled to play the piano for his host. Robert called in his wife, Clara – herself a concert pianist – to hear the young visitor play. She beheld such a marvelous beauty of tone and Brahms wanted to be held by such a marvelous epitome of beauty. Meanwhile, Robert was beholden to write a marvelous epic tome in *Neue Zeitschrift*. His article was well meaning, and praised Brahms to the sky, but inadvertently pitted him against the mighty Wagnerite peons.

Brahms almost always had to confront obstacles strewn in his path, and he never secured an official conducting post in his native country. (Practically everyone in Music Hystery could have warned him about that.) He finally had to go to Austria and became conductor of the Vienna *Singakadamie*. There he learned why he was never accepted as a conductor in Germany – he was lousy at it. But his music left a big impression on Vienna – especially the *Liebeslieder* and his monumental *German Requiem*, dedicated to the memory of his mother.

Beyond Clara Schumann (his 'ideal maternal'), Brahms's outlook on women was slightly chauvinistic. He viewed them under the three K's: *'Kinder, Kirche, Küche,'* or 'children, church, kitchen.' Women thought this reprehensible and saw Brahms

under the three S's: '*Schrecken, Schmerzhaft, Schrecklich,*' or 'fearsome, painful, awful.'

While rehearsing the oratorio *The Creation,* Brahms admonished a few of the elderly ladies in the choir as he lay down his baton: "Why do you drag it so? Surely you took this much faster under Haydn?"

Brahms experienced hefty mood swings and would insult whomever he pleased – although he didn't please very many by insulting them. The young composer Hugo Wolf once sent Brahms a song and asked him to mark a cross wherever he thought it was lacking. Brahms sent it back and said: "I don't want to make a cemetery of your composition." Wolf was not crazy about this response and has since proclaimed:"Brahms' music is a celebration of impotence ... he is like a departed spirit that returns to its old house, totters up the rickety steps, turns the rusty key with much difficulty, and directs an absent-minded gaze on the cobwebs that are forming in the air and the ivy that is forcing its way through the gloomy windows." No wonder Wolf went insane as a composer – he missed his calling as a ghost writer.

Brahms travelled everywhere. In Germany he was greeted with great relish by Hamburgers and Frankfurters, and afterward, Hungary. During these travels, an old friend by the name of Henschel caught Brahms on a good day: "Brahms, rather stouter than I had ever seen him before, was in the merriest of moods and did ample justice to the excellent beer of Munich brew, of which he consumed an astounding quantity."

After all his successes, Brahms never forgot Schumann's kindness with that first article. When Schumann died in 1856, Brahms raced to Clara's side and offered his support for 40 years. How ironic that at her funeral in 1896, he should catch a cold from one of the mourners and die a short time later.

With his symphonies, Brahms wanted to be next to Beethoven.With his *Lieder*, Brahms wanted to be next to Schubert. Brahms got his wish: He's buried next to both.

Camille Saint-Saëns
b. Paris, France, 1835; d. Algiers, Africa, 1921

With a name like Saint-Saëns (pronounced 'See-Saws') it was most unfortunate he had a lisp – ethpecially around the time he wath writing hith thecond thymphony.

By the age of 10 his tinkling was so accurate at the keyboard he could play all 32 of Beethoven's piano sonatas from memory. When he was 13 he was accepted into the Paris *Conservatoire.* He loved to stand in its courtyard and listen to "the desperate squawking of sopranos and tenors, the trilling of pianos, the honking of brass, and arpeggios from the clarinet, producing a cacophony of noise which avant-garde composers try desperately to create without much success."

Saint-Saëns accepted the position of organist at the *Madeleine* – a fashionable church in Paris where *haute couture* was far more important than High Mass. One of the priests actually begged him to lower his musical taste to the level of their philistine parishioners, but fortunately, Saint-Saëns was a rude man and knew how to tell priests where to go.

Many church organists are atheists and Saint-Saëns was no exception. When the pistons kept failing, the Lord's name was heard more from the organ loft than the chancel. Since he didn't believe in Hell, he spent a lot of time looking at heavenly bodies. (He certainly didn't find them at the opera.) Saint-Saëns bought himself a telescope (for an astronomical sum) to look at the stars. He also gazed across the city to get an eyeful of various Paris sights. Speaking of parasites, he began peering across the city to see what his rivals Massenet, d'Indy and Franck were composing. (This is known as peer pressure.) His favourite student, Fauré, occasionally went up to the roof after a lesson with Saint-Saëns as a constellation prize. It was Gabriel's first foray into the galaxy.

The musical politics in Paris at this time were practically worse than the political politics. A famous cantata competition was held in 1867 (the year Canada became a country – I thought I'd sneak that in) and every known composer in France entered. Many of them used *noms de plume* to sign their works because they had gone through the politics before. First prize was given

to Saint-Saëns, and Berlioz – his friend and jury-member – wrote to congratulate him. For a million undisclosed reasons, the authorities decided not to have the winning cantata performed, and it was replaced by the *Hymne a Napoléon III* – a work written by Rossini, who happened to be from another country. He also happened to be one of the jurors.

Saint-Saëns escaped to another country in 1871, for France was engaged in civil war. He sowed many seeds in London, England, and was the inaugural performer of Albert Hall's new pipe organ. True to form, England championed this brilliant French musician for many years, whereas France always challenged him.

In 1875, Saint-Saëns married a girl half his age and produced two boys. Tragedy struck when the eldest boy leaned too far out a window and fell four stories to his death. The other boy – a sickly child – died six weeks later. Saint-Saëns left his wife to fend for herself three years after their bereavement. So much for the 'Saint' part of his name.

The composer Massenet was up against Saint-Saëns to be a member of the prestigious Institut. Human nature wound up making Massenet the outright winner as he was indescribably wealthy and didn't speak his mind the way Saint-Saëns did. The triumphant member wrote to the rejected one: "Dear sir, the *Institut* has made a grave injustice." To which Saint-Saëns replied, "I completely agree with you."

The composition for which Saint-Saëns is best known is *Carnival of the Animals* – a work in which stampeding children turn the concert hall into a zoo. The many movements turn instruments into different kinds of animals, and Saint-Saëns, cleverly re-orchestrating various works of contemporaries such as Offenbach and Berlioz, probably turned their stomachs.

After the success of *Carnival of the Animals* – a turning point in his life – Saint-Saëns made a beeline for the Canary Islands. He checked into the trendiest hotel under a false name and talked to no one. Other vacationers started playing games as to who this nebulous character was. A chambermaid spied on him as he was jotting down strange hieroglyphics on paper. Everyone decided he must have been a secret agent and called the police. Saint-Saëns realized he was under surveillance and must have thought Massenet was spending a fortune to see what this new composition was all about.

In 1891, nearly 20 years after he had written the opera *Samson et Dalila*, the Opéra finally decided to have it produced. Its enormous success proved it to be on the cutting edge of dramatic opera. (He should have hired the Barber of Seville to cut Samson's hair for an even bigger hit! A bad idea, actually, especially since Saint-Saëns' and Rossini's close shave in the cantata incident.)

Saint-Saëns kept on travelling to forget his wretched past. He returned to Paris to give his take on Debussy's music. Because he was afraid of it, his lisp became more pronounced as he said to a friend: "I thintherely dethpithe *Pelleath et Melithande*." Saint-Saëns was never very impressionable anyway.

Modest Mussorgsky
b. Karevo, Russia, 1839; d. St. Petersburg, Russia, 1881

Mussorgsky's mother started teaching him piano at a very young age, and even taught him a difficult concerto by the Irish pianist John Field, when he was only nine. So Mussorgsky's proud *mamushka* was able to say to her neighbours that her little boy was outstanding in his Field!

Even with all this adulation, he became modest in demeanour – although if too harshly criticized, de meaner Modest became. As we have seen in the rest of Music Hystery, if one has any hint of talent, one is going to be unduly chastised for possessing such an aberration. In later years, Mussorgsky's masterpiece *Boris Godunov* was written of in this manner: "Mussorgsky, through his ignorance and desire to be novel and egregious at all cost, has achieved barbaric, hideous results." Oh well, Mussorgsky had an excuse. As a youth he was a lazy little bugger, which is why he spent so much time standing in fields. He had such a late start in music that by the time he was 18 he had composed only one polka. (He didn't meet as many girls as Smetana.) To be fair, Mussorgsky tried to write an opera when he was 17 but had no idea what he was doing. Instead, he gave up and joined the Russian army.

In 1858, Mussorgsky had a nervous breakdown. (Perhaps as a musician, joining the Russian army is never a good idea.) Within the year he visited Moscow and was truly inspired as a patriot. To celebrate this happy revelation, Mussorgsky started a symphony, which he never finished, and then he decided not to complete an opera. This frenzy of eschewed activity lasted about five years – on and off. His teachers Balakirev and Stasov rarely agreed with one another, until they talked about Mussorgsky: "He is, I think, a perfect idiot," said one (or the other). Mussorgsky would have appreciated this, for he was always striving for perfection.

Mussorgsky became infatuated with an OPERA SINGER (they are always larger than life) named Latysheva, but he was a little shy once it was known that he had a 'congenital malformation of the sexual organs.' *Pictures of an Exhibitionist* would have been an inappropriate title, so Mussorgsky wrote

Pictures at an Exhibition instead (the piano version, that is. Ravel later pounced on the work and out-Russianed the Russians with his indulgent French orchestrations).

Mussorgsky contemplated marriage — musically speaking, that is, for he wrote a work called *The Marriage*. It contains the first examples of *leitmotifs* in Russian music. But instead of Wagnerian content such as Wotan-like gods, magical swords and women with humungous breastplates, Mussorgsky wrote tunes for noisy children, a barking dog and a canary. Then he started work on *Boris Godunov* and that other famous Russian — Smirnoff. By 1873, Mussorgsky was dividing his time between the ink bottle and the vodka bottle. (He discovered the vodka was tastier and didn't make his tongue go black.) He also partook in heavy smoking, and his friends couldn't abide the ferocious hacking. "Just a cough-itch," Mussorgsky would say, but his friends knew that Shostakovitch wasn't due till the next century.

Finally, Mussorgsky was turfed out of his apartment — practically penniless (rubleless?). "What is a composer without a flat key?" thought Mussorgsky, and then he died.

No one could leave his works alone. Rimsky-Korsakov happened along and 'corrected' his music posthumously (that is to say, after *Mussorgsky* had died). In life, Mussorgsky was ungrateful toward the Russian master. He said of Rimsky-Korsakov: "Even in cloud-cuckoo-land you would not expect to find artists so indifferent to the essence of life ... so useless to contemporary art."

Speaking of useless, Mussorgsky left much of his work unfinis-

Pyotr Ilyich Tchaikovsky
b. Kamsko-Votinsk, Russia, 1840;
d. St. Petersburg, Russia, 1893

Tchaikovsky's most famous works include *The Nutcracker Suite* (too suite for some), *Sleeping Beauty* (which people loved but couldn't stop yawning), and the *1812 Overture* (high-calibre stuff – especially with the cannons, giving the crowds more bang for their buck, or rumpus for their ruble).

Thanks to his dad, Tchaikovsky started his career as a government clerk. One day, as he was dreaming about sugarplum fairies, young Peter absent-mindedly tore up and ate an important document while listening to someone in his office. His father began thinking music wasn't such a bad profession after all.

During the composition of his first symphony, Tchaikovsky was hallucinatory (he believed he was a fairy) and the doctor ordered him to take a *lunga pause*. He became entranced by Désirée Artôt – a Belgian soprano, whose career in London (not Brussels) sprouted – and marriage was considered.

Marriage to Désirée was not to be, but Tchaikovsky was adamant. He told his brother and sister that he would be married very soon – even though not a single prospect was in sight. He finally fell in love with a woman named Carmen, but she turned out to be only an opera (and besides, she was too Bizet for him).

Suddenly, the ideal woman appeared – or at least, didn't appear. She was no hallucination, she was Nadezhda von Meck, a wealthy eccentric who wanted to give Tchaikovsky enough money to live so he could concentrate on his compositions. One stipulation was they were never to meet. Now, is this an ideal woman or what?

Tchaikovsky was still longing to be married, with no purse-strings attached. This he did, to the chagrin of those in his family who knew he had swung the wrong way. Her name was Antonina, a stupid and delusional girl who became committed to Tchaikovsky *before* the asylum. From the start she unwittingly drove him nut-cracking mad to the point where he wrote von Meck asking for money to get away from his new wife. A charming honeymoon.

TCHAIKOVSKY'S 'NOTECRACKER'

Meanwhile, Tchaikovsky had written four symphonies and was at work on *Eugene Onegin* – an opera about a man who was deceitful in love and got his comeuppance in the end.

A couple of weeks after Tchaikovsky had introduced Antonina to his friends and family, he waded into the icy River Moscow to catch his death (not to catch fish, as he told his wife later). But the only thing that really got wet was his dampened spirit when he came out of the river not dead.

It took some time before Antonina granted him a divorce. Tchaikovsky could now breathe a little easier in his new country home at Klin – some 50 miles from Moscow. Tchaikovsky began to regain some calm after his failed marriage and started travelling. He was treated like a king in the major capitals of Europe and met with such composers as Busoni, Dvorak, Fauré, Gounod and Massenet. (So fastidious was Tchaikovsky, he actually met them in alphabetical order.) Of all these composers, Massenet was his least favourite because 'M' doesn't appear on the keyboard.

In 1890, Tchaikovsky wrote the opera *The Queen of Spades,* which contains more storyline of unfulfilled love. Curiously, the scene he added into the story has the tragic heroine throwing herself into a canal when she realizes her boyfriend isn't interested in her. Obviously, the guilt over the loony Antonina was resurfacing in spades.

Then something really horrible happened: Nadezhda von Meck cut off Tchaikovsky's salary and made the excuse she was bankrupt. He knew she wasn't, and it plagued him for the last three years of his life because he didn't know the real reason. In a fit of despair he drank a glass of unboiled water and died of cholera. When his brother was asked why he did such a thing, he replied: "Peter picked a Meck of fickle rubles."

Antonin Dvorak
b. Nelahozeves, Czechoslovakia, 1841;
d. Prague, Czechoslovakia, 1904

Little Anton apprenticed with his dad as a violinist and pork butcher. He grew up in a small village inn that attracted many kinds of peasant folkmusic, usually accompanied by a *pesante* (heavy) style of dancing.

In 1853, Dvorak journeyed by wagon to Zlonice, near Prague. He brought everything – including his violin – accompanied by his father. It was a fair distance, and there were a lot of double and triple stops before they got to the bridge.

In Zlonice he learned the viola, organ, theory and earned a little money as sub-organist in an insane asylum.(A lot of musicians seem to end up there one way or another.)

Dvorak fell in love with a 16-year-old actress named Josefina Cermáková, who was not in the least bit interested in him, so he married her younger sister instead. (Anna was the singer in the family anyway.) By this time, Dvorak had written a lot of stuff – including two symphonies and a few operas. He wanted to maintain a national character, as Smetana had done. He discovered an interesting national character when he wrote an opera called *The Pig-Headed Peasant*. (I wonder if he had to convince his pork-butchering father it wasn't biographical?) To make up for it, he later wrote *The Cunning Peasant*.

The formidable Brahms 'discovered' Dvorak after the latter submitted his *Moravian Duets* to the Austrian government in search of a grant. Brahms introduced Dvorak to the famous publisher Simrock, who published most of his works. Simrock wanted morav Slavonic and lessov Moravian, for it was the popular *Slavonic Dances* making all the money.

Dvorak became famous and began sketching his *Stabat Mater*. Sadly, two of his children died in quick succession and Dvorak finished the work not feeling his usual self – which is why the *Stabat Mater* sounds a lot like Verdi.

In 1892, Dvorak was invited to New York by a rich grocer's wife to become the director of the National Conservatory, but he was tremendously busy writing three overtures, conducting his works in England and breeding pigeons at home. (No, the Dvorak

family was never *that* hungry – but they were cold, and needed the pigeon droppings to fuel their stove.) At this point, it occurred to him it was definitely time to move to New York – the place was covered with pigeons! The amount of heat would be phenomenal! And the offered salary of $15,000 a year wasn't bad either.

Once in New York, the Dvoraks wanted to go home – they were homesick and they were boiling because of all that pigeon poop. (Dvorak commented that he never wanted his statue erected in New York – he would have been splattered beyond all recognition.) They decided to visit a Czech colony in Spillville, Iowa, of all places. It was here he made sketches for his most famous work – *The New World Symphony*. Dvorak loved the native music of America and fused it with his own. Another example of this intermixture is the well-loved *Nigger Quartet* – (meaning, there are a lot more black notes than white) – which, of course, was not as offensive then as it may be today.

Upon his return to Czechoslovakia, Dvorak was always looking for literary material that would represent his people. He wanted to set to music the *Ant in the Dwarf-Shack* – based on a Czech folk tale – but it sounded too much like his name. Instead, he came up with a comic opera called The *Devil and Kate* and a tragic one called *Russalka*.

Dvorak travelled the world, but nowhere was he better loved than England, where he conducted his works in the most important halls. The Brits loved his quaint, simple nature so much they sold pictures of him in their storefront windows – and they went like hot-cakes. After a while, the sales slowed down – most shoppers thought it was a portrait of Jack the Ripper.

Nikolai Rimsky-Korsakov
b. Tikhvin, Russia, 1844; d. Lyubensk, Russia, 1908

Rimsky-Korsakov came from a family of sailors and felt compelled to write a lot of music in and around the high Cs. While he was with the Sea Cadets, he made up a chamber choir of 18 voices, which sang choruses mostly from Glinka's operas. Much to his dismay, authorities decided to acquire a band and disband the choir. (I presume there weren't enough naval basses.)

Nikolai became professor of composition at the Conservatory of St. Petersburg. He had been heavily influenced by Berlioz and in 1868, invited the French composer to conduct six concerts for the Russian Music Society. Berlioz was sick the whole time – to the point where he got his animal metaphors confused, as disclosed in his diaries: "I've been ill with 18 horse-power coughing ... like six donkeys with the glanders." The next year, Berlioz died. (I blame Mr. Rimsky-Korsakov for having assisted in the premature death of one of my favourite composers. You read it here first, folks.) With Berlioz out of the way, Korsakov felt compelled to usurp the master by writing his *own* treatise on orchestration – which has since become as much of a classic as Berlioz's. (You see – there's even a motive.)

A dissertation could be written based on the fact that Rimsky-Korsakov shared a single room with Modest Mussorgsky in 1871. They penned their respective operas – *The Maid of Pskov* and *Boris Godunov* – at the same table. Imagine the cross-pollinating possibilities. It would have been interesting if a window had been left open, allowing a strong breeze to mix the two piles of manuscript. Both Russian *and* Music Hystery could have benefited from the revision of this current event.

In 1872 Rimsky-Korsakov married Nadezhda Purgold. He struck the mother lode in Purgold, as she was a beautiful woman and proved to be a better pianist than he. There couldn't have been a more suitable person to arrange all of his works for piano. (Hmm ...perhaps the *marriage* was arranged for the piano as well.)

Rimsky-Korsakov belonged to a group of Russian composers called 'The Five' – which consisted of some of the most important composers in the country, making them quint-essential. Even

94

so, he couldn't stop himself from deriding his fellow musicians: "Owing to deficient technique, Balakirev writes little; Borodin slowly; Cui perfunctorily; Mussorgsky untidily and often non-sensically." I have to add here that Rimsky-Korsakov writes redundantly: He spent much of his time writing other composer's works. Not only did he 'correct' Mussorgsky's harmonies and voice-leading, he also had the audacity to orchestrate Schubert, Handel, Glinka and Borodin's monumental opera, *Prince Igor*. (Thank God he redeemed himself by writing *Flight of the Bumblebee*.)

In 1882, Rimsky-Korsakov met a very enthusiastic and extremely wealthy amateur musician by the name of Belayev. When word got out that Belayev celebrated each new chamber composition with a never-ending supply of bubbly champagne, there was suddenly a never-ending supply of bubbly Russian quartet music.

Rimsky-Korsakov wasn't very interested in chamber music – not with Berlioz as a mentor. In 1888, he wrote his most famous work, the symphonic suite *Scheherezade*. He also wrote 15 operas. Then he heard Debussy's opera *Pelléas et Mélisande* at the *Opéra-Comique* in Paris and said: "I will have nothing more to do with this music, or I might unhappily develop a liking for it." In other words, he was jealous, and sensed that Debussy had pushed the annals of Music Hystery forward, as Rimsky-Korsakov had done from Berlioz. The usurper usurped – and by a French composer, no less.

Rimsky-Korsakov went back to his teaching and stuffy academia, where he knew he was safe from any young pretentious upstarts. In 1906, a young man peered into his office and asked if he could take private lessons. "Of course, lad, what is your name?" "My name, sir, is Igor Stravinsky ..." Rimsky-Korsakov died shortly thereafter – and later became known to thousands of schoolchildren as: Nikolai Rips-his-corsets-off.

Edward Elgar
b. Broadheath, England, 1857; d. Worcester, England, 1934

Sir Edward Elgar was a bit of an enigma to his fellow countrymen. For many years his talent went unrecognized because jolly old England has always had a nasty habit of snubbing those who are not of very high social standing. Elgar's father owned a small music shop in a small village and never discouraged little Eddie from choosing a life as a musician. How disgraceful.

Elgar thus became bandmaster at the County Lunatic Asylum when he was just 22 years old. This experience undoubtedly put him in good stead for the future, when he would have to deal with professional musicians.

In 1886, Elgar married Alice Roberts, a very understanding woman who made life a lot easier for an aspiring composer. Not only would she prepare his tea and meals for him, but also his manuscript paper by marking bar lines and names of instruments – and when nicely cajoled, would fetch his slippers and roll over and play dead. Even these wifely, consolatory duties couldn't quite pep up the beleaguered Elgar. It wasn't until his famous *Enigma Variations* did the little island prick up its ears and stiffen its upper lip. The English also had to conceal their embarrassment for not heretofore acknowledging a genius in their mist. (As a belated apology to the entire population of England, I have to say that Elgar was unrecognized by his fellow countrymen because he wrote a load of rubbish until he was 41 – owing to the fact that he was largely self-taught.)

Elgar's mind was easily distracted. One of his best friends, a violinist named William Reed, was surprised to find himself being dragged off to the racetrack. They bet on a horse because its name – Semiquaver (the English equivalent of a 16th note) – suggested a quick tempo. The horse won and Elgar went back to the track many times. The music world should now be indebted to those racetrack horses whose names were Hope and Glory.

Sir Edward enjoyed the simple things in life. He flew kites, threw boomerangs, went fishing, played pool and indulged in chemistry sets and carpentry. By all accounts he wasn't very good at any of them. He had to run like hell from a pursuant

boomerang, he caught microscopic fish, accidentally blew up his garden, and actually built for his sister a double bass, whose grizzly bear sounds made his dogs howl.

He returned to his composing and wrote one of the great English oratorios – *The Dream of Gerontius* – whose premiere on October 3, 1900 at the Birmingham Festival was a total disaster. Aside from its technical difficulties for the amateur singer, not enough preparation time had been spent. To make matters worse for subsequent performances, the work is based on Roman Catholic doctrine, which doesn't go over very well in the Church of England.

Lady Elgar died in 1920. This blow left Sir Edward with no compunction for counterpoint. His friend William Reed tried everything to get him composing again. While walking through the streets of Gloucester, they played a game that required spotting bearded men. The first to do so had to yell "Beaver!" to score a point. A red beard meant three points. For old Elgar and his concertmaster, yelling "Beaver!"throughout the streets of Gloucester was fun for a while but it wasn't enough to get the creative juices flowing, and before he made it back to his compositions, Elgar had developed a brain tumor.

The BBC commissioned a third symphony from him but he couldn't finish it. As Elgar lay dying he made his daughter Clarice and William Reed promise that no one should touch the sketches. They promised. As of last year, Elgar's *Third Symphony* can be heard in its entirety. The man who finished it should know there is a warrant out for his arrest, and his artistic licence will be revoked.

Elgar enjoyed the music of Wagner, Berlioz, Schumann, Schubert and Liszt – but one of his favourite recordings had a song with the words: "Mucking around the garden, good old uncle Joe."

Giacomo Puccini
b. Lucca, Italy, 1858; d. Brussels, Belgium, 1924

Judging from his birthdate, Giacomo was one of those unfortunate kids who received a gift and was told it was a birthday and Christmas present wrapped up in one. He was a lazy little boy, and failed most of his exams every year. He took music lessons with his uncle, Fortunato Magi, who kicked him in the shins whenever he sang a bum note. It is known that years later, whenever Puccini heard a sour note, he would react by sending his foot up into the air with a jerk (the jerk being his uncle Magi).

Puccini's first stint in the performing arts was as organ bellowist (for want of a better term) for his church organist. One day, he and his little atheist friends took off with some organ pipes so they could buy cigarettes and candy. They were caught and reprimanded by the organist, who told them how bad all that candy was for their teeth. (Puccini was caught stealing later in life when he had become a world-famous composer: He was tried in court as a poacher and the judge was terrified of having to convict one of Italy's heroes – so he didn't. Saved by a hare, no doubt.) Inspired by the organist, Giacomo himself acquired an organ post at St. Martino and St. Michele, Lucca. He no longer ate any candy but he smoked like a chimney.

It was a performance of Verdis *Aïda* at Pisa that made a towering impression on Puccini. He knew from this point what he was leaning towards – he wanted to be an elephant trainer. No, not really. He wanted to be a famous operatic composer. Puccini's first opera of any note(s) was *Manon Lescaut*, with a libretto by Illica and Giacosa, among others. These two men would provide the composer with text for the next three operas. In return, Puccini provided his librettists with much pain and anguish, perhaps just to see how these human emotions were played out so he could translate them into music. *La Boheme* was the opera to follow. The critics were for the most part, disparaging: 'It will fail to leave any strong trace in the history of opera,' or 'What was it that turned Puccini into the deplorable downward path of La Boheme?' etc. A later performance in Rome proved to be so successful that the death scene, of all things, was repeated. Mimi had to be exhumed from her dressing room.

100

I'd like to interrupt this shopping list of operas to announce Puccini's marriage. The lucky girl who had to withstand a lifetime of infidelities was Elvira Bonturi – a non-musician, so nothing more is to be said about her. (Most of these infidelities were not Puccini's fault – one ravishingly stunning woman actually showed up on his doorstep stark naked. What was a young, handsome, Italian, Romantic operatic composer to do? More research, I suppose.)

Tosca was the next biggie to premiere and there were rumours of a bomb scare. (It may have been the critics again, hoping for *Tosca* to bomb.) But the only ugly incident was the police yelling at latecomers. (What a great idea – they should also arrest coughers and candy-wrap extricators.) In 1904, *Madame Butterfly* had a disastrous premiere at La Scala in Milan. Puccini was pissed off and hissed off the stage. Perhaps the audience found the love interest between an American and a Japanese geisha girl disorienting; perhaps there were too many occidentals. Who knows? *Turandot* was Puccini's last opera. He didn't quite finish the last 36 pages (how is it known the number of pages he didn't complete? – a little sketchy, I'd say) and the work was completed by someone else à la Puccini mode – that is to say, with scoops of Neapolitan sixths aplenty. Yum!

Puccini died of throat cancer brought on by eating too much candy. His favourite pastimes were fishing, hunting and power boating.

Gustav Mahler
b. Kalist, Austria, 1860; d. Vienna, Austria, 1911

When Mahler was five years old he was asked what he wanted to be when he grew up. "A martyr," was his answer.

For a time when Mahler was a student, he roomed with composer Hugo Wolf, who started going insane shortly after an argument with Mahler. A friend of Wolf's, Hans Rott, also went insane after having met Mahler. (Come to think of it, Mahler's friend, the painter Gustav Klimt, was mad as a hatter. I wonder if there was a destructive force at work here.) When Max Steiner, a student of Mahler, went to Hollywood and wrote the soundtrack for *King Kong* (about a top banana lured to the Big Apple and subsequently destroyed), was he thinking of his revered teacher? When Thomas Mann wrote the novel *Death in Venice* (with Mahler in mind as the principal character, who remains in Venice and is subsequently destroyed), was he thinking of his revered friend as a propagator of self-destruction? Only his psychiatrist, a certain Dr. Freud, would have known for sure – but psychiatry in those days was still fairly Jung.

Understandably, Mahler entered into his *Ninth Symphony* with great trepidation. Most composers died after penning their ninth symphonies as a kind of unwritten musical rule. Beethoven, Bruckner (well, Schubert nearly made it) and Dvorak called it quits after their ninth, so Mahler procrastinated by turning his ninth symphony into a symphonic song cycle entitled *Das Lied von der Erde*. Finally he had to give in and write it anyway. He was dead angry when he felt well enough to start his 10th.

But let us return to his early years. He fell in love with Johanna Richter (a young nurse? – no; a tobacconist? – uh-uh; a dark-haired singer? Bingo!!) A short-lived relationship with Johanna inspired the song cycle *Songs of a Wayfarer*. Elements from these songs made it into his precocious first symphony.

While he had a conducting post in Leipzig, Mahler had an affair with an older woman who happened to be the wife of Carl Maria von Weber's grandson. This episode nearly became as scandalous as some of the operatic plots he was forced to conduct. He nipped this in the bud and escaped to Budapest.

After three years of pulling up the socks and putting bums

in seats for the Royal Opera House in Hungary, Mahler still felt the effects of Semitic sematics. Most critics scoffed following a performance of his first symphony, (most of the audience coughed during) but it was a German critic with the unlikely yet soothing name of August Beer who admired his efforts. Undoubtedly, Mahler became homesick for German Oktoberfests and obtained a position in Hamburg for six years.(Beer goes well with hamburg.)

It was in Hamburg that Mahler met Bruno Walter, a 17-year-old musician who was witness to Mahler's most famous quote as they were climbing a spectacular-looking mountain together: "Don't bother looking up there," Mahler said. "I've composed that already."

Another soprano appeared on the scene – the seductively gifted 23-year-old Anna von Mildenburg, who stood on the coat-tails of Mahler (he was only 5'4", so this was possible) all the way to Vienna.

Mahler was told he'd never get a position in Dresden, Berlin, Munich or Vienna unless he was a Catholic, so he converted to Catholicism and got the job in Vienna. This didn't stop the bass Theodor Reichmann from privately calling Mahler 'the Jewish monkey.' Another singer, Schmedes, was filled with praise for Mahler – and filled with beer, for Mahler invariably had to fetch him from the pub in time for rehearsals.

Mahler married in 1902. The woman was Alma Schindler, who was compulsively drawn to genius. The men she captivated and captured were some of the most important in Austrian society. Hence, Schindler's list: two painters, two musicians, one architect, one writer, a soldier, a tinker; a tailor and a spy. Alma was completely devoted to Mahler and gave up a promising musical career so she could spend his money.

New York did indeed lure Mahler and paid big bucks for him to stand on a podium and wave his arms about – just like King Kong. But the state of his empire building came crashing down because of a fatal throat infection.

As Mahler lay dying with Alma at his side, a fierce thunderstorm raged, like the one during the death of Beethoven. Alma was afraid of any lightning activity, for Mahler was such a good conductor.

Claude Debussy
b. Saint-Germain-en-Laye, France, 1862;
d. Paris, France, 1918

"He was the poet of mists and fountains, clouds and rain." In other words, Debussy lived in a sort of haze. And no wonder – he smoked like a chimney. "The virtuosity with which he rolled a cigarette in glueless paper without spilling the minutest speck of tobacco was a source of wonder and admiration to great and humble alike among the Parisians he encountered daily." Truly a man with inestimable talents.

He was a bit of a rebel at the Paris *Conservatoire* and was always marked down in class because of his incessant parallel bars (harmony class, not gym class) of fifths and octaves – the very thing that made him famous. Debussy also loved to make fun of the compositional tendencies of his professors, and chastised his friends for playing traditional cadences. He would call this: "Falling into the arms of the old lady." Of course, at the *Conservatoire*, it was nothing but 'old ladies' to which the students were exposed.

In 1884 Debussy won the *Prix de Rome*. Like his fellow compatriots in previous chapters, this won him a spot in the Villa Medici for three years. It was in this very villa from 1630-1633 where Galileo himself had been imprisoned for his outlandish theory of the Earth revolving around the sun. The only difference between this great astronomer and these young French *artistes* was their belief that the world revolved around *them*.

Debussy couldn't stand Rome and left early. In 1887 he lived with Gaby 'of the green eyes' Dupont. Debussy loved anything green. He loved green so much he had green chairs and tables, green carpets and wallpaper, and walked with a green cane. Apparently, his kleptomania was limited to anything green, and he was seen shoplifting a green tie. Anyway, back to Gaby. She discovered he was being unfaithful and decided to punish him by shooting herself. In the end she wasn't a good shot, recovered from her injury, and returned to live with him. He opted to punish himself by leaving Gaby to marry someone else. Her name was Rosalie Texier. Again, he made the mistake of choosing someone who didn't appreciate his infidelities. When

Rosalie discovered he was far more interested in the rich wife of a banker, she too shot herself – and missed. Debussy felt badly about all these women shooting themselves and waited almost a year before he married Emma, the banker's wife (a singer ... yawn), but not before having a little girl whom they called 'Chouchou.' (She didn't arrive on time.)

In the 1880s Paris was gripped by Wagner fever. Debussy had no time for this long-winded German, and composed delicate little cream-filled confections. Parisian *poseurs* caught on to Debussy's delicate ways of thinking and began calling themselves 'Debussyists,' to distinguish themselves from the 'Romanticists.' They even fashioned their hair like his – a kind of pre-Beatle mop. Then he discovered the perfect French play, which he wanted to make into an anti-Wagnerian opera. It was Maurice Maeterlinck's *Pelléas et Mélisande.* He hired the author to write the libretto and the two got on very well. Debussy spent eight years on the opera and finally played it for Maeterlinck, whose wife, the singer/actress Georgette Leblanc, had to poke him to keep him awake, for this was French Impressionism at its subtlest. Debussy eventually gave her the role of Mélisande (presumably, because she knew how to keep her audience from falling asleep) and started rehearsals with her. In the meantime, the director of the opera had given the role to someone else. Maeterlinck and Leblanc read about this in the paper and took Debussy to court. The composer won – sort of, in spite of a slight altercation where Maeterlinck burst into Debussy's apartment with popping veins and a big stick. Debussy spiraled downward in a dead faint, as did 'Pelléas' at the box office. "A curious experiment," said Rimsky-Korsakov of the opera.

The Afternoon of a Faun – an orchestral tone poem of 1894 – changed the idea of rhythm and colour in music and practically made the bar lines melt.

But it was always works for the piano where Debussy excelled. When the audience heard the world premiere of Debussy's famous piano piece *Cathedral Under the Water* in 1910, there wasn't a dry seat in the house. Indeed, it is the aural equivalent of waiting for a Monet painting to dry – at least, that's *my* impression.

Richard Strauss
b. Munich, Germany, 1864; d. Garmish, Germany, 1949

Strauss was a composer who lived on the residuals of beer. His mother's family were the owners of the famous Pschorr brewery. His father was an accomplished horn player who actually locked horns with Wagner and other celebrated conductors. Thanks to his wife, he could afford to.

The girl Strauss married was no fading violet either. While conducting a rehearsal with orchestra and soloists, Strauss found his head to be the recipient of a thrown score, compliments of Pauline de Ahna – an enraged soprano. He followed her into her dressing room and the orchestra was horrified by the shrieks emanating from it. Then silence. The musicians must have wondered whose head was going to roll out the door, but they would have to wait for Strauss's opera *Salome* for that one. Finally, out came Strauss with the tamed soprano, and happily announced their engagement to the stunned orchestra.

A few years after the marriage, Strauss wrote a tone poem entitled *Sinfonia Domestica*. It was a depiction of his married life with Pauline and their new baby. One critic called it "one of the most embarrassing works in the history of music [sic]. One can practically hear the clearing away of breakfast dishes and the Strauss baby crying its head off." (No, no – that's *Salome*.) Hans Richter said that the gods in burning Valhalla did not make one quarter of the noise that one Bavarian baby made in the bath – or was that Pauline throwing scores about the house? For some strange reason, the work required an orchestra of massive proportions, (and a Simon Rattle).

It was the symphonic poem in which Strauss reveled as a master orchestrator. *Don Juan* was the first that brought him to the fore. Unfortunately, it was *Eine Alpensinfonie* that brought him to the aft – a miserable failure. In between was *Also sprach Zarathustra*, which brought him into film, (like his namesake Johann, this music was featured in Stanley Kubrick's *2001: A Space Odyssey*. See caricature) and *Ein Heldenleben* – a bombastic tone poem depicting his own 'heroic' life. (*Henpeckedleben* would have been more appropriate.)

In 1898, Strauss signed a 10-year contract with the Royal

Opera House of Berlin. His fame was secured and he made a healthy enough income to compose opera. *Salome* was ready for the picking.

The Irish writer Oscar Wilde had written the play *Salome* in French, which was subsequently translated into English. Strauss read a German adaptation of it, was pleased with the material but not the adaptation, and asked one of his friends to translate it from the English into German again. I can only guess Strauss loved employing circles of fifths within his harmonic progressions to keep up with the metamorphic text.

When his father heard *Salome* at the keyboard, he said, "it sounds like a swarm of ants crawling in the seat of your trousers." But the opera was a sensation, and swarming audiences crawled into the seats of the great opera houses to hear it. In 1907, the newspapers of New York screamed, "abhorrent, bestial and loathsome ..." "... the most horrible, disgusting, revolting and unmentionable features of degeneracy I have ever imagined ..." Of course, after all this great free press, ticket prices doubled and it took dozens of policemen to control the enthusiastic crowds. Other operas to follow were *Elektra, Ariadne* and *Der Rosenkavalier*.

Strauss once hailed a cab. The driver asked him "where to?" Strauss said, "it doesn't matter, I'm in demand everywhere."

The aging composer was certainly in demand by the Nazis, who needed internationally famous men like Strauss to legitimize their cause. At first Strauss endorsed Hitler and his merry men but realized things were not kosher when they tried to prevent Stefan Zweig – one of his collaborators, and a Jew – from working with him. Strauss said all kinds of things that would have sent any common man to his death (he even called Wagner's *Tristan* – one of Hitler's favourites – "as tiring as a steady diet of lobster mayonnaise"). But when it came to politics, Hitler realized Strauss didn't know his brass from his oboe.

Strauss was once asked by a reporter: "What are your plans for the future?" His response: "I plan to die."

The legacy of Richard Strauss's music and Pschorr beer lives on.

Jean Sibelius
b. Tavastehus, Finland, 1865; d. Järvenpää, Finland, 1957

His symphonies have been called 'antediluvian monst-rosities.' However, he became so famous abroad due to his *Finlandia* that when Russia attacked Finland in 1939, the American people were introduced to a stamp bearing his likeness with the words 'I need your help.' He single-handedly carried a fervent nation – musically speaking – into the 20th century. No wonder he had to relax for 30 years.

Of course I am speaking of Jean Sibelius. Until Sibelius, there hadn't really been a Finnish symphonist of any note (not one whose name was pronounceable, anyway) because in 19th-century Finland, they would have had to comb the bush in search of people who could play an orchestral instrument.

But let us start from the beginning. When Sibelius was 11 years old, his mother enrolled him in a Finnish-speaking grammar school. (Most schools were Swedish-speaking.) It was here little Jean learned the epic story of the *Kalevala* – the story of Finnish mythology that had arrived on the scene in 1835. Having been in thrall by the Russians and Swedes, the Finns were enthralled by the emergence of a Nationalistic movement toward the end of the century and the *Kalevala* was a watershed of folklore from which writers, painters and composers drew inspiration, and collectively redefined their culture.

Sibelius was at the forefront of this movement and the Finns followed every move of the hero in his *Lemminkäinen Suite*. Such titles *as Lemminkäinen and the Maidens of the Island*, *The Return of Lemminkäinen*, *Lemminkäinen Skips to the Loo* and *Lemminkäinen Flagellates after the Sauna*, kept everyone on the edge of their pine-hewn chairs.

Sibelius was a practical man. He wrote for whatever instruments were available, which means he wrote infrequently. Chamber music was the answer, and he sent a number of these compositions to Brahms, hoping the old man would take him on as a student. Unfortunately, Brahms was too busy staring at Clara Schumann's bosom and didn't want to teach anyway.

In 1891, Sibelius wrote the *'Kullervo' Symphony* – a massive Mahlerian work that assured his place in the annals of Music

Hystery. But there were critics in some quarters who thought Sibelius too old-fashioned, along the lines of Brahms or Elgar. Indeed, the height of his powers paralleled the New Viennese School of Schoenberg et al (ban Berg). It is easy to understand a group of young, restless, limelight-hungry Viennese intellectuals jumping onto an atonal bandwagon. Somehow, sitting in the middle of lush forests for 90 years isn't exactly conducive to a calculated, abstract, jagged-edged style of writing.

In 1892, Sibelius married Aino Järnefelt, whom he had ordered through the Ikea catalogue, and they lived the rest of their days in Järvenpää, an idyllic little place surrounded by nothing but trees and double-dotted accents.

Sibelius agreed to be the first director of the Eastman School of Music, which had just opened in Rochester, New York. He later declined, regarding it as unfinnish business to attend to.

The symphonic work *Tapiola* was Sibelius's homage to the myth and nature of his country. So Nordic-sounding, so evocative of the Finnish landscape, it was apparent from the very first line which part of the world it had come from. (He had, however, written it in Italy.)

Sibelius was not very highly thought of in Germany or France (if he was ever thought of at all). They were too busy warring among themselves under the auspices of the Wagnerites vs. the Debussyites, and an unknown composer from an unknown country entering unannounced into the Ring was a gross indecency. He had already squeezed the most nutritional bits out of both country's best composers, and he had changed his name from Janne to Jean without France's permission.

The English may have championed Sibelius because he had made France and Germany so mad – so much so that Winston Churchill sent him several cigars for his 90th birthday out of sheer gratitude, and to wish him good health. *Gesundheit* and *merci*, Jean Sibelius.

Erik Satie
b. Honfleur, France, 1866; d. Paris, France, 1925

"Gifted but sluggish, passable, mediocre, feeble, worthless, can't sight read properly, the laziest student in the *Conservatoire*." An auspicious beginning for Satie, who became one of the first minimalists – having done a minimal amount of work in school.

He must have put more energy into the titles of his music than the music itself. Here are a few examples: *Three Pieces in the Form of a Pear*; *Flabby Preludes* (for a dog), and *Dessicated Embryos* – a great name for a feminist rock band.

After his extremely short stint at the Paris *Conservatoire*, Erik went to work playing piano in a cabaret in the Bohemian part of the city. This life-style brought him into close quarters with very strange friends. One of these friends was a would-be inventor who designed things such as the 'necromobile'. Half car, half crematorium, this phantasmagorical machine would incinerate the freshly dead, providing enough fuel to propel itself to the cemetery in time for the interment of the ashes. What a wonderful way to go, (and you wouldn't have to pay for gas.)

Satie was one who countered anything that took art too seriously – or anything German. (Yes ... Wagner yet again.) He joined in the fight with his friend Debussy against the pedantic breast-beating of Romanticism, and was suspicious of anything that reeked of commercialism. (Satie would have feigned consternation at the thought of the number of tv commercials and films in which his music has appeared.)

True to Bohemian form, Satie refused to write a set of piano pieces for a publisher until it was agreed he should get paid *less* money. (The publisher didn't have to feign consternation – he must have thought he was an idiot). The publisher agreed, and Satie happily went about the task of writing *Sports and Diversions*, based on a series of jocular watercolours.

Possibly his most famous works for piano are the placid, yet strangely moving *Gymnopédies*. These are minimalistic pieces which mystified many but attracted the likes of Debussy to its mysticism. It has been said of the *Gymnopédies*, "they must have been written by a savage with taste." Satie also wrote *musique*

ERIK
SETTEE

d'ameublement, or 'furniture music' which, I'm sure, many musicians would like to rearrange. He also introduced a typewriter, an airplane engine, and other paraphernalia into his orchestra for a more 'modern' sound.

One day, in 1893, Satie met Suzanne Valadon, a model for Renoir, Degas and Tolouse-Lautrec, (she was known to be a little too loose herself) and that same evening he asked her to marry him. Suzanne was already the mistress of a wealthy young lawyer but she moved into the apartment next to Satie anyway. Here is an endearing quote from the composer after he got to know her a bit better: "She has a tender little belch which is often inspiring."

Satie met Cocteau in 1915. Together, with all the artistic Bad Boys of World War I, they created *Parade*, which had a music hall influence. Satie wrote the music for Diaghilev's *Ballet russes* and Picasso designed the sets. A known French critic vehemently damned the performance. Satie felt compelled to write: *Sir and dear friend. You are nothing but an asshole, and an unmusical asshole to boot. Erik Satie.* A libel suit ensued, and Satie was sentenced to eight days in prison. He had now entered the mainstream of Parisian artistic life, and lived for just over a week in a space that was probably no more austere than his own.

Satie was the type who wrote his music one bar at a time. Namely, at the *Chat Noire*, the *Brasserie Pousset*, the *Chez Weber*, etc. It was in these establishments he would bump into Debussy and other lubricated composers.

He became the 'spiritual daddy' of *Les Six* – a group of French composers who pretty much revolted against everything except their own work. Even then they began revolting against each other. In the end they were just simply revolting.

A friend said of the composer: "Satie was against Wagner in 1885; against Debussy in 1905; against Ravel during the war, and against *Les Six* just before his death. I think this is wholly admirable."

Ralph Vaughan Williams
b. Down Ampney, England, 1872; d. London, England, 1958

Ralph (pronounced 'Rafe') Vaughan Williams was born into a family that had evolved from Charles Darwin – the controversial fellow whose ideas firmly discounted the story of the first existing man and woman. (Of the Bible, Darwin couldn't give A dam and Eve'n dispelled the notion of the first man and woman ever having belly-buttons). 'Uncle Charlie' must have had some influence on the young Ralph as he went on to contemplate his naval activities in WWI.

From a man whose world evolved, to one whose world revolved, Vaughan Williams became best friends with the creator of *The Planets*. I'm referring, of course, to Gustav Holst. (Not who you were thinking.) Holst could write rings around other composers – especially when he was writing *Saturn*. As an example of their musical correspondence, (and a different sort of revolution) Vaughan Williams once wrote to Holst: "... heard Tchaikovsky's 1812 at Queen's Hall the other day. I've never heard such a row. Band, organ, bells and someone apparently hitting a tub."

Another interesting association in RVW's life was that his first marriage was officiated by the Rev. W. J. Spooner – the man who 'wixed up his murds' with such constant hilarity. This form of dyslexia became known to the world as Spoonerisms. One can imagine Ralph and Adeline's wedding ceremony: "Do you make this tan to be your waffly-leaded husband?"

Not to be outdone by the fertile imaginations of Bartok and Kodaly (who motored from rural village to village collecting tunes that were practically springing from their soiled countrymen), Vaughan Williams pedaled around the countryside capturing English folksongs. Afterward, he would go back to his church organ and pedal till he was worn, then hand his freshly notated music to the publishers so they could peddle the wares for the till.

Aside from studying with English composers such as Stanford, Parry and Wood (Stanford was actually from Ireland, but England's best composers were usually Irish), Vaughan Williams went to Paris and studied with Ravel, who asked him

to *'écrire un petit menuet dans le style de Mozart'*. Vaughan Williams basically told the French composer to shove some manuscript up his chunnel: He wasn't coming all that way just to write like some dead, famous composer – no matter how dead or famous he was. Vaughan Williams and Ravel became very good friends after that.

RVW wrote a great deal of choral music – especially music for the sea (or is that coral music?). Works such as the *Sea Symphony* and *Five Tudor Portraits* were always favourites at the Three Choirs Festival in Gloucester – an event in which he enjoyed taking part. (Some of his own ensembles back home in Dorking sounded quintessentially English and even somewhat obscene: Imagine taking part in Dorking Oriana or the Dorking Madrigal choirs)?

Later in life, RVW was visiting an American university, and agreed to listen to a piano composition by one of the star music students. After listening to a half hour of tortured dissonance, RVW thanked him and said, "If by chance a tune should occur to you, dear boy, don't hesitate to write it down."

Sergei Rachmaninov
b. Semyonovo, Russia, 1873; d. Beverly Hills, USA, 1943

Rachmaninov's family had been well off for many years, until the father gambled away four of his wife's estates. Then for some inexplicable reason, they separated. Little Sergei was brought up by his grandmother, who basically let him do whatever he wanted. He decided he didn't want to practice piano too much and replaced this inactivity with terrorizing the neighbourhood. Meanwhile, his sister was a beautiful pianist and contralto who attracted many boyfriends. Sergei and his grandmother sat around hedging their bets as to who was going to get the girl. (This gambling trait obviously stemmed from the father.)

Sergei was on the road to slothville if he didn't do something fast. It was suggested that he become a student of the famous teacher Zverev in Moscow. This he did, but it meant actually living with the master and two other boy pupils – a situation which today's society might think of as a little more than 'tickling the ivories.' But it worked out for the best. Zverev was well-respected in Moscow – he was buddies with someone called Tchaikovsky – and made a lot of rubles teaching and gambling at cards. (Where does this gambling end?)

The young pianist improved tremendously because of Zverev and was becoming exposed to some of the greatest Russian musicians of the era – including those in the "Belayev Circle" – Glazunov and Rimsky-Korsakov, among other lesser known St. Pete types. The Belayev Circle was named after a wealthy lumber merchant whose philanthropy made music in Russia as rich in timbre as he made Russia rich in timber. Sergei later said of Korsakov: "It seems strange that a man who handled the secrets of the orchestra in so masterful a fashion, down to the smallest detail, should be so helpless as a conductor."

It was the inept conducting of Glazunov, leading the premiere of Rachmaninov's *Symphony No.1* which put the composer into a three-year depression. He was at such War with himself that his friends tried everything to keep the Peace. Appropriately enough, they invited Leo Tolstoy to snap him out of it. A novel approach.

Rachmaninov was very close to his family. He married his first cousin – Natalya Satina – in 1901, and eventually had two girls.

The Russian people created a bit of a rivalry between Rachmaninov and another great pianist/composer/mystic theosopher – Alexander Scriabin. Rachmaninov was astonished that Rimsky-Korsakov agreed with Scriabin's theories in that certain colours were connected with musical keys, but they didn't really agree upon which colour went with which key. The more they argued, the more they yelled at each other: Korsakov: "No! F sharp major is blue!" Scriabin: "Is not" Korsakov: "Is too!" Rachmaninov: "Nyet. Nyet!" etc. By the end of the argument, Scriabin had turned red and was screaming in D major, Rimsky-Korsakov was blue and screaming in C# minor, and Rachmaninov ... various shades of purple in E flat.

Rachmaninov became a mega-star as a pianist, conductor and composer – especially with his four piano concerti. The Russian border guards were so thrilled to have the great man and his family at their gate during the end of WW 1, they waved tearful goodbyes to the Rachmaninov's as they escaped the country.

They finally settled in sunny Beverly Hills, California. Perhaps Sergei and another import, Arnold Schoenberg, had a few pool-side gin and tonics together and talked shop. On second thought, Arnold would only have had the gin – never the tonic.

Arnold Schoenberg
b. Vienna, Austria, 1874; d. Los Angeles, USA, 1951

Just when everyone thought Wagner had taken the break down of tonality as far as it could go, Arnold Schoenberg (not to be confused with that other famous 20th-century Austrian artist, Arnold Schwarzenegger) came along and had a *complete* break- down. He brought this affliction on himself, as he was a self-taught composer.

His friend Alexander von Zemlinsky, a famous conductor, helped produce a number of projects for Schoenberg, as did his sister Mathilde, who helped produce a couple of children after she married the fertile composer. Richard Strauss was another major influence on young Arnie; a letter of recommendation from this great symphonist resulted in a couple of scholarships. But when Schoenberg sent him some of his music, Strauss couldn't figure out which way to hold it. The old master approached the young composer and asked if he was a Wagnerian or a Brahmsian. Schoenberg replied: "No, I'm a Selfian." Strauss later commented to a friend: "I think he'd be better off shovelling snow than scribbling on music paper." Schoenberg proved him wrong by moving to California.

Mahler also tried to defend Schoenberg, and personally admonished individuals who were mocking his music, even though he didn't have a clue what Schoenberg was up to. The latter composer once explained how one could use varying instrumentation of a single note to achieve a kind of melodic event. Mahler thought Schoenberg was out of his mind, but kept lending him money in the hopes that he would go after another kind of professional help. (Mahler could have suggested Sigmund Freud, since he himself had already been one of his couch potatoes.)

Schoenberg spent a number of years working on what became known as a 12-tone row, which essentially obliterates any trace of a tonal centre. (Arnold could have been useful to the CIA.) It was given other names, too: the 12-note row, dodecaphonic music, serialism, atonality, and names that are unfit to print – even in this book. Two of Schoenberg's students, Anton Webern and Alban Berg, became disciples of this new approach

to music. Berg left sand in Webern's face by writing *Wozzeck*, a psychologically taxing opera written in atonal fashion. This raised Berg's mantle in Music Hystery and he is no longer regarded as 'just another one of Schoenberg's students.' – like Webern.

The premiere of one of Schoenberg's most famous atonal works, *Five Pieces for Orchestra,* took place in London, England. According to the critic Ernest Newman, only a third of the audience hissed at the work, because another third was too busy laughing; the last third seemed too nonplused either to laugh or to hiss. Newman goes on to give Schoenberg some credit for not being the lunatic he thought he was.

The audience reaction in England couldn't come close to the one in Prague when *Pierrot Lunaire* was performed. Schoenberg's take on these 21 poems contained a double-whammy. Not only are they completely atonal, but he created a technique he called *sprechstimme* – a kind of 'speech-singing' that permeated the work. Upon hearing the caterwauling (which to an untrained ear sounds not unlike a constipated mongoose in heat – come to think of it, that's what it sounds like to a trained ear as well), audience members went bonkers and created their own caterwauling through *sprechstimme*, adding fisticuffs to the mix. Throughout the evening, police had trouble keeping the people in czech.

Not surprisingly, one of Schoenberg's biggest fans was Adolf Loos, a deaf architect.

One of the international editions of *Who's Who* lists Schoenberg's hobbies as bookbinding, tennis and ping-pong. One of his noisiest opponents in ping-pong was Harpo Marx.

Charles Ives
b. Danbury, USA, 1874; d. New York, USA, 1954

Charles Ives's father George was a bandleader (not in the aboriginal sense) who was involved in that historical event of the most oxymoronic – the 'Civil' War. As a boy, George was found secretly picking cherries in order to buy a flute. He should have done what his namesake and former President did – cut down the whole dang tree. (Washington could have bought himself a whole orchestra with all those cherries, but wound up just using the wood of the tree to fashion a pair of dentures.) It was George's unorthodox method of listening to music that set his son on a path of polytonality (a tricky path to wander down because there are so many tuning forks in it). But Charles was to prove himself a master at negotiating the many deviant curves in both music and business.

Young Charles's first composition was a memorial to his dead cat Chin-chin. This was followed by a passacaglia in honour of his dead dog. Funereal disease set in and he started writing for several other dead neighbourhood animals. Ives was now known for writing on a pet-a-tonic scale.

He watched his father build a contraption that could play quarter tones – a great instrument for accompanying those who enjoy singing in the cracks. (Years later, in 1925, in a definite nod to his father, Ives set up a 'quarter-tone' concert, which caused great hilarity on the music scene.) Just to give an idea as to George's sensibilities, he once said that Haydn and Mozart were "two pretty boys of music."

Like his father, Charles had what's known as perfect pitch. (And in 1894, he defeated Yale as pitcher for Hopkins Preparatory School's baseball team.) Ives quickly became one of the most respected businessmen in the United States – another blip on Music Hystery's landscape. He rose to be the head of the Raymond Agency, which was to become the biggest insurance agency in the United States. (He has since Met his match in a dog named Snoopy, who works for peanuts.)

In 1908, he (Ives, not Snoopy) married a girl with the very melodious name of Harmony Twichell – a good friend of Mark Twain. (But could she sing?)

Ives wrote very technically difficult music, which "needs more than one set of ears to hear." Now and then, an American folk tune pokes its way through the polyharmonic texture – making everything OK again. In his evocative *Orchestral Set No. 1*, or *Three Places in New England*, one movement depicts two marching bands as they come toward each other, pass and then move away from each other. (Ives had created stereo before it was technically possible.) The clashing effect is spectacular, and can be described as several accidentals looking for a place to happen.

Much of Ives's music was deemed as unplayable in his time, as Beethoven's music was in his. Ives didn't hear most of his music until he was retired. Beethoven didn't hear *any* of his music when he was retired.

Ives was a generous soul: He didn't want any royalties, nor did he want his publisher to make royalties – he just wanted his music out there. Once the general public got to hear it, the verdict was unanimous: Ives's music is definitely out there.

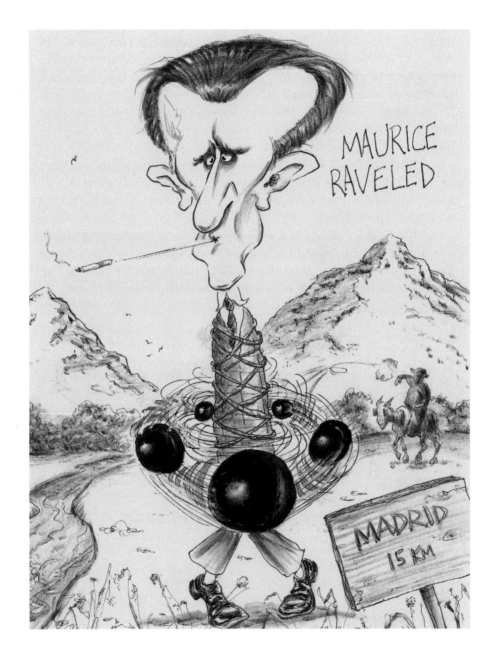

MAURICE
RAVELED

MADRID
15 KM

Maurice Ravel
b. Ciboure, France, 1875; d. Paris, France, 1937

For a composer, Maurice Ravel had an unusual childhood – it was a happy one. His mother was a Basque from Spain, his father a Swiss engineer and inventor who may have invented the first internal-combustion engine, and a car that could turn somersaults. The latter didn't go over well.

Ravel studied with Fauré and was inspired by Satie, Debussy and the Russian Nationalists. He entered the Paris *Conservatoire* at the age of 14 and for 16 years tried to win the *Grand Prix de Rome* – not in a somersaulting car, but in composition. He was rejected so many times for the award it nearly started another French Revolution. The Parisian intelligentsia reveled in this public scandal, which became known as *'l'affaire Ravel.'* The number of letters fired across the city finally 'un-Raveled' the head of the *Conservatoire* and he had to resign.

Paul Wittgenstein, the one-armed pianist, single-handedly made it fashionable for 20th-century composers to write piano concerti specifically for the left hand. (How gauche. But cymbals would have been more interesting.) Among the composers who went out on a limb were Prokofiev, Hindemith, R. Strauss and Britten – so naturally, Ravel thought he'd try his hand at it.

After that little novelty had worn off, Ravel returned to writing for musicians with two arms. Some of his more famous works are *Jeux D'eau*, for piano; the *Mother Goose Suite*; and *Pavane*, of which there are many arrangements.

Ralph Vaughan Williams studied with Ravel. The French composer told the Englishman not to write such heavy Germanic music and gave him Russian music to orchestrate. In 1907, Ravel went into his Spanish period, eventually writing his master piece *Daphnis and Chloe*, based on a Greek tale.

Finally, the work that needs no introduction. Just as Mendelssohn roused the world with Bach's *Passion According to St. Matthew*, it was Bo Derek who aroused the world with *Bolero*, and the *Passion According to Dudley Moore*. Ravel said of *Bolero*: "It is devoid of music." That may be so, but it sure sold tickets, and posthumously, Ravel can basque in his own glory.

Bela Bartok
b. Nagyszentmiklós, Hungary, 1881; d. New York, USA, 1945

The great late conductor George Solti said of Bela Bartok: "I never heard any gossip about him; he was absolutely pure, like a saint." This makes things very difficult for a satirist – especially when one takes into account Bartok's plethora of illnesses and impoverished life – very poor fodder indeed. So let's take a look at his mudder ...

One day, Bartok was teaching a pretty young student by the name of Ditta while his mother was preparing lunch. It seemed a rather long piano lesson, or so Mrs. Bartok thought, when Bela came in to the kitchen and said "Ditta will be staying for lunch." The lesson resumed in the afternoon and went on for hours until Bartok informed his mother that "Ditta will be staying for dinner as well. And by the way," he said, "we're married." Apparently, Bartok was furious when a close friend, upon discovering this secretive marriage, wrote a note of congratulations. Based on this incident, one certainly cannot accuse Bartok of blowing his own horn (he hired musicians to do that for him). His character, one may presume, can be summated as unassuming. However, it is noteworthy that his notation is not without notoriety. As an example, his ballet *The Miraculous Mandarin* contained the stuff that nightmares are made of.

Three pimps coax a girl to dance at the window of a dingy, decrepit room to attract men from the street. After a couple of victims are lured, robbed and chucked out, the Mandarin enters and is both bewitching and repugnant to the girl. She resumes her erotic dance until he starts chasing her about the room. The three villains ambush and suffocate him but he refuses to die. They stab him again and again and hang him from the ceiling, the blood gushing to the floor until he finally dies. (Not exactly happy hour with Lèhar or Rossini.) The cheery libretto of *The Miraculous Mandarin* was provided by Melchior Lengyel, who eventually emigrated to the United States and became a Hollywood scriptwriter. Opera simply wasn't violent enough for him.

Bartok and fellow composer Zoltan Kodaly visited the countryside with a hand-cranked phonograph. He had peasants

stick their heads into the cone and sing their little tunes so that they were imprinted onto a wax plate. (In effect, Bartok was fashioning an aural wax museum – a bit like Graumann's Chinese Theater, where the stars make their imprints in concrete, then fade into oblivion.) In the end, Bartok had sorted and categorized 13,000 Hungarian melodies and folk music from other countries. To his countrymen, he was a national hero; to other composers beyond Hungarian borders, he was a glorified librarian. (Game shows such as *Name That Tune* would have been tough going in Hungary).

France recognized Bartok's 50th birthday by making him 'Chevalier de la legion d'honneur.' The Hungarian authorities had to make a belated albeit sheepish attempt to match this by awarding him the Corvin Wreath. It is interesting to note that Berlioz was constantly snubbed by French authorities, but was lauded as a hero by the Hungarians. This attitude is known as cultural free trade.

In 1940 Bartok and his wife went to New York, where the violence in the streets was slightly less than Europe at that time. Here he wrote his most famous work – *Concerto for Orchestra* – which pits the various sections of the orchestra against one another. Whoever could utter the most Balkan-sounding tunes before the end of the concerto won.

Apart from six string quartets, Bartok wrote three highly entertaining and innovative piano concerti. And as one can see by the highly innovative and entertaining caricature, he learned his lessons well from one of Liszt's students.

Bartok was born at the wrong time for two reasons: (a) the world wars kept interrupting his folksong collecting, and (b) another half-century later and he could have played those 13,000 tunes into a midi-based computer.

Igor Stravinsky
b. Oranienbaum, Russia, 1882; d. New York, USA, 1971

Stravinsky was known as a chameleon in music. He wrote a violin concerto in a quasi-Bach style, *Pulcinella* in a quasi-Pergolesi style, and music for the church, complete with bells, in a quasi-modal style. (No wonder Disney wanted him.)

Rimsky-Korsakov took him on as a private student because he was already too far behind for the conservatory. Stravinsky benefited tremendously from this master orchestrator and wrote a splashy piece called *Fireworks*. Serge Diaghilev, the flamboyant impresario of the Paris-based *Ballet Russes*, heard the work and asked Stravinsky to write a ballet for his company. The result was the *Firebird,* which charmed audiences and made Igor instantly famous.

Petrushka followed in 1911 with Nijinsky dancing the title role. Diaghilev was ecstatic and premiered yet another Stravinsky ballet within two years. With *The Rite of Spring*, Stravinsky and the *Ballet Russes* garnered infamy *en famille*. No one was quite ready for the explosion that has kept the Hystery of Music smoldering to this day. That reminds of a true incident connected to this spectacular opening-night debacle: A couple of American music professors visiting Paris that May 29, 1913, looked at the evening paper and wondered what they should attend – a new work by Igor Stravinsky, or the *Folies Bergères*? (I'll answer that later). In *The Rite of Spring*, Stravinsky had created the primitive musical equivalent of a pagan ritual, where wise elders sit in a circle with torches and watch a girl dance herself to death (similar to the *Folies Bergères*). At the premiere, the audience heard and saw some of the strangest things coming from the stage and started to riot. The Parisians were screaming and punching their neighbours and became even more primitive than what they had paid to experience. Because the evening had not gone quite as planned, the composer later violently attacked the choreography. It's too bad Stravinsky hadn't been placed on stage during this tirade – Diaghilev would have witnessed the savage realism he had been looking for. (The profs, by the way, opted for the *Folies Bergères*.)

World War I broke out – but *The Rite of Spring* had nothing

to do with it, although it's rather suspicious that Stravinsky took off for Switzerland. He lived there for six years with his wife and children. (Earlier, he had married Catherine Nossenko, his first cousin.) In the meantime he wrote *Five Easy Pieces* (nothing to do with Jack Nicholson) for two pianists. In Switzerland he extended his knowledge of numbering bars to numbered bank accounts.

In 1917 Stravinsky met Picasso as he was reigning on Satie's *Parade*. They were similar in going through many noteworthy 'periods' – excluding male menopause. Each dabbled in Neo-Classicism, a Blue(s) period, and, later, cubism. (That's when Stravinsky called his fellow composers "blockheads.")

Picasso went to a post-performance party *après Pulcinella*. The show's success had been intoxicating and so was the party. Other guests included Diaghilev, Cocteau, Poulenc and Princess Eugène Murat. Stravinsky got plastered, grabbed all the cushions he could find, and started a major pillow fight. Too bad Satie hadn't been there. He could have supplied appropriate furniture music.

In 1921 Stravinsky moved his family to France, where he met Vera de Bosset, who was connected with the *Ballet Russes*. She became his mistress but didn't marry him until 1940, after Catherine had died. The moral here: Don't marry your first cousin.

In 1940 Walt Disney's *Fantasia* hit the screen, with *The Rite of Spring* depicting dinosaur sequences, which Stravinsky thought despicable. Hollywood beckoned again, commissioning him to compose a *Circus Polka* for P.T. Barnum that featured several dancers and 50 baby elephants. Stravinsky would do anything for money, and found himself writing for tu-tus and tusks. Tsk, tsk.

In 1948 Stravinsky met Robert Craft, who became a kind of professional diarist, advisor, confidante, catsitter and substitute conductor until Stravinsky's death. Craft's *Chronicle of a Friendship* is a remarkable catalogue of the cities and people they visited, including Khrushchev, JFK, Eliot, Huxley, Auden and Chaplin. Craft also introduced Stravinsky to some Schoenberg, whose academic system of music he hated. (Schoenberg died just a stone's throw from Stravinsky's house – but it wasn't Stravinsky who cast the stone.) In the bathroom of an airplane, Stravinsky once secretly wrestled with sheets of toilet paper to figure out a 12-tone row for a new work. But as the plane touched down, the triumphant Stravinsky was able to put all that work behind him.

Sergei Prokofiev
b. Sontsovka, Russian, 1891; d. Moscow, Russia, 1953

Little Sergei was the type of precocious kid you hoped got the super-wedgie at camp. When he was nine he wrote his first opera. At 13 he was accepted into the St. Petersburg Conservatory and inflicted his conceit on everyone under that roof for the next 10 years.

Needless to say, he met few friends during those years except for Nikolai Myaskovsky, who was 10 years his senior. They played a lot of chess together – a game that undoubtedly taught Prokofiev how to manipulate pawns, which benefited him during the Stalin years.

Prokofiev loved to play the role of the *enfant terrible* and shocked people with his modern piano compositions. He never let his *avant-garde* down. Forced to play something other than his own works – something drab like Schubert or Mozart – he made sure to 'improve' it by adding what he thought must surely be missing.

Even though he was well hated at the conservatory, they gave him the coveted Rubinstein award and a grand piano, hoping it was enough to keep him away from the school for good. (Some wanted to award him with the piano from the second floor – but that's another story.) They were wrong. As soon as WWI broke out, Sergei enrolled again. It was obvious he was more interested in manuscript paper than conscript paper.

Prokofiev wrote an opera called *The Gambler,* which began rehearsals in 1917. True to the violent nature of the work, the participating artists threatened to mutiny: The singers and musicians (I mean the instrumentalists) despised their parts and the director resigned. A revolution followed – the February Revolution of 1917 – but it wasn't Prokofiev's fault. Although he liked confrontation in music, he wasn't keen on war, and moved to America in May of 1918.

The Gambler could almost be applied to Prokofiev the composer/impresario. Producing opera is like playing a one-armed bandit, and out of the 10 operas he wrote in his life, Prokofiev finally hit the jackpot when three oranges came up. The unlikely name of this winning opera: *The Love for Three Oranges*. He

nearly died while writing this work (allergic to fruit, perhaps) and the fellow who was to conduct it dropped dead before the premiere. Prokofiev decided to try his luck in France, and went searching for healthier conductors.

Prokofiev began writing his famous ballet based on Shakespeare's *Romeo and Juliet* in 1934. He felt in a bit of a quandary by the time he got to the end because he didn't think the pair should be dying and still dancing. (Why can't someone mention this to the opera world?) *Romeo and Juliet* was put on ice (so to speak) until Prokofiev came up with the best way to dispose of them. (He should have gone to Stalin for advice.)

He finally moved back to Russia in 1936 and found that the government now had control as to the artistic and social content in music. One of Prokofiev's operas was about to be staged, and again, another little setback: His producer was arrested and executed. It was getting to the point where Prokofiev was attending more funerals than opening nights.

He wrote *Peter and the Wolf* around this time, a charming children's tale scored for chamber ensemble and narrator. Prokofiev must have been furious when Stravinsky – whose guts he hated – had his infamous *Rite of Spring* animated by Walt Disney, whereas *Peter and the Wolf* was initially rejected (a form of suspended animation).

In 1938 Prokofiev met up with Mira Mendelson – a literary student half his age. Their relationship broke up his marriage to Lina Llubera, a Spanish-born singer he'd married in 1923, and later nearly destroyed Lina. Mira was known to move about in powerful circles, something that Prokofiev came to appreciate. Interestingly enough, Lina was arrested in 1948 – the same year Sergei and Mira were married – and was sent to labour camps for nine years, allegedly for espionage. Game of chess, anyone?

Ultimately, the music of the spheres converged with the hand of Fate on March 5th, 1953, and took the lives of both Prokofiev and Stalin. The deranged despot disposed of his composers even in death – and knocked poor Prokofiev from the front page of every newspaper in the world.

Prokofiev's piano works (including five concertos) may have shocked and disturbed his countrymen, but at least he didn't kill 20 million of them.

140

George Gershwin
b. New York, USA, 1898; d. Beverly Hills, USA, 1937

Gershwin is probably the only one in Music Hystery who started out as a street punk. It's hard to imagine the likes of Frederick Chopin beating the crap out of some miscreant in the slums of New York, but this is how the I-got-plenty-o'-nuttin' life of George Gershwin began.

Just like a character right out of *West Side Story*, George fell in love with music when he was playing stickball in the streets and heard the sweet strains of Maxie Rosenzweig's violin through an open window – or at least a smashed window. He quit school at 16, learned how to play the piano and started work at Tin-Pan Alley – a place that was a veritable pop-song factory. Pianists were assigned a cubicle and played all day long for clients in search of the next show-stoppin' tune. George hated the drudgery of banging out songs and longed for the simpler things in life – like banging heads together in the ghetto.

After some success of having a few of his songs performed alongside composers such as Bartok, Hindemith and Schoenberg, (which is about as bizarre as the jazz clarinetist, Benny Goodman, commissioning a work from Bartok) another of Gershwin's works, an experimental one-act Negro opera, was performed by – and I blush at the irony of the name – Paul Whiteman and his orchestra. Whiteman was so pleased with the work that he advertised in the *New York Tribune* a new major symphonic/jazz work by George Gershwin. The first time Gershwin knew about this was when he bought a copy of the paper. George called Whiteman and complained about the short notice, threatening not to write the new work. Whiteman told Gershwin that if he didn't write it he would grab him by the by the throat until he turned – and suddenly Gershwin was inspired. Within three weeks he wrote *Rhapsody in Blue*.

While travelling through Paris, Gershwin dropped in on Maurice Ravel, wanting to take composition lessons. Ravel admonished him, saying: "Why do you want to become a second-rate Ravel when you are already a first-rate Gershwin?" Stravinsky was his next choice as teacher. He eyed the young New Yorker and asked: "How much do you earn from your music,

George?" "Oh, about two hundred thousand a year," Gershwin replied, and Stravinsky said, "Then maybe I'll come and study with *you!*"

Gershwin was itching to create something on a large scale. He had plans to write *Corgy and Bess,* a three-act opera set in Buckingham Palace about the relationship between the Queen and her pets, but it didn't pan out. He knew he had to think of something a little closer to home – something that would speak the language of the simple American folk.

Then the idea struck him. Why not Porgy and Bess? – the story of a crippled Negro beggar (nowadays he would be considered a physically and monetarily challenged person of dusky hue) and his love for Bess. George took off for Charleston, South Carolina, to get in touch with the rich musical idioms of the black South. With famous tunes such as *It Ain't Necessarily So* and *Summertime, Porgy and Bess* became an American operatic masterpiece. Gershwin went on to enjoy tremendous fame – and became as black as Michael Jackson is (or became) white.

Dmitri Shostakovich
b. St. Petersburg, Russia, 1906; d. Moscow, Russia, 1975

"In hockey, the puck is too small – I can hardly see it. I like football best." This proclamation comes from the lips of Dmitri Shostakovich – one of the most important composers of the 20th century.

Secretly, he desperately wanted to become a referee for a Leningrad soccer league. Imagine if this behemoth of a musician had favoured a sporting career as opposed to writing 15 string quartets and the same number of symphonies! But thankfully, Shostakovich had Coke bottles for glasses, which made his eyes appear like two large saucepans – precluding any kind of foray into the world of adjudicating athlete's feet.

At 13, he was accepted into the Petrograd Conservatory. The well-known composer Glazounov was headmaster at the time, and was so impressed by Shostakovich's talent he gave him a grant from the Borodin Fund. This fund was financed by receipts of Borodin's opera *Prince Igor*, and of course, those who received this money had to be Godunov for Glazounov.

In 1928 Shostakovich completed his first opera, entitled *The Nose*, based on a story by Gogol. *The Nose* was picked by a committee at the Malily Opera Theatre, and it opened there in 1930. Happily, Shostakovich's *Nose* ran in Leningrad for many, many weeks.

A more famous opera was *Lady Macbeth of Mtsensk*, completed in 1932. Its premiere was praised profusely and lauded as a great nationalistic work, until the daily *Pravda* damned it as vulgar and neurotic. Suddenly, not a Russian soul defended Shostakovich and the opera languished in a metaphysical Siberia for a quarter of a century. After her return from exile, *Lady Macbeth* was hypo- critically hailed as a masterpiece for a second time – but at least Dmitri was beginning to face brighter Prospekts.

In the meantime, Shostakovich alternated between writing a piano concerto and music for an animated cartoon called *The Tale of the Priest and His Helper, Dolt*. In 1939, he wrote for another cartoon entitled *Tale of the Stupid Mouse.* Other anomalies among his *oeuvre* included music for a movie called *Girlfriends*, and a very entertaining arrangement of the popular tune *Tea for Two*.

The Nazis invaded the USSR in 1941 and disturbed Shostakovich as he was composing. This made him really mad – his *own* country was allowed to threaten him with death, but not any other. As bombs exploded and machine-gun fire pierced the air, Shostakovich wrote the *'Leningrad' Symphony* and dedicated it to the besieged city. The score was microfilmed and flown to America through war-torn skies – into the hands of Toscanini. His NBC Symphony Orchestra played the work on radio for millions of listeners. The music is tricky enough, but it must have been difficult to play from such a teeny-tiny score.

As Handel was writing the *Hallelujah Chorus*, a servant apparently witnessed the great man with tears streaming down his face, saying, "I have just seen the heavens open and a host of angels singing a song of praise." Shostakovich had a similar reaction composing his *Eighth String Quartet*, but was somewhat more prosaic: "While I was composing it, the tears just kept streaming down like urine after a half-dozen beers."

Russian composers tended to write for the lower register of the keyboard so that pianists from their country had the distinct characteristic of leaning toward the left. This was especially good for the Communist judges' vantage point in big piano competitions. Shostakovich, who in later years eventually lost the use of his right hand, had to conform to the left anyway. Fortunately, there were already in existence a few piano works written especially for the left hand. Benjamin Britten had written one for a fellow who – it was discovered later – had only a right hand. The situation was rectified by a bit of judicious re-fingering and placing the pianist on his head. These two composers, who were admirers of each others' work, shared the same cause – Pacifism. Shostakovich wrote many 'war' symphonies, and Britten wrote the *War Requiem*. For two Pacifists, they sure created some of the loudest music known to Man (enough to wake the dead).

Speaking of which, the Stalin purge had smoked out many of the Russian intelligentsia, who were subsequently executed. Shostakovich must have infuriated Stalin by virtue of remaining alive for so long – he was just too bloody famous to get rid of. Eventually, Shostakovich was one of the few Soviet artists to die from natural causes – smoke and vodka inhalation. Well, natural enough for a Soviet artist.

John Cage
b. Los Angeles, USA, 1912; d. New York, USA, 1992

Whereas Berlioz reveled in the thought of 800 horns or harps even *before* a slight indulgence in opium, John Cage (a member of the Czechoslovakian Mushroom Society) settled on writing for anything short of the toilet or kitchen sink, even before his indulgence in magic mushrooms. Fellow American composer Aaron Copland said of Cage's work: "Those who enjoy teetering on the edge of chaos will clearly be attracted."

Amplified toy pianos, water-filled conch shells, radios, whistles, rainsticks – these are some of the instruments Cage called upon for his curiouser and curiouser works. How about this one from 1962: *0'00" – solo to be performed in any way by anyone*; from 1972: *Bird Cage – 12 tapes to be distributed by a single performer in a space in which people are free to move and birds to fly*; or from 1975: *Lecture on the Weather – 12-speaker-vocalists, preferably American men who have become Canadian citizens, with tape and film*. If Cage had thought of this last piece about a decade earlier, there could have been a myriad of performances with all those draft-dodgers. Oh well, timing is everything.

So who is this John Cage? And was he really as scary-looking as the caricature on the next page? (The French press actually wrote that Cage was reminiscent of a sweet-looking Frankenstein.) Cage's father was an inventor who made improvements to the internal combustion engine (remember, it was Ravel's dad who practically invented it) and went bankrupt because another business development wasn't as airtight as it should have been – he was working on a submarine, and with it sank his good fortunes and wet dreams.

Cage's student years were as unorthodox as the rest of his life. During the Depression, in Santa Monica, California, he went door to door to see if housewives would bandy together and pay $2.50 for 10 lectures on modern art. Forty housewives bandied. Aside from the abstract works of Piet Mondrian, Cage was exposing them to his teacher, Arnold Schoenberg, or at least to his serial music. (One wonders, after hearing this music, how many of these women became serial killers.)

Since these biographies are mercifully brief, I think Cage's "micro-macrocosmic rhythmic structure" phase can be omitted here so we can move on to his most famous creation – the 'prepared piano.' This was accomplished by inserting objects next to the strings of the piano, such as nuts, screws and bolts. I must digress here, because I have just remembered that I have forgotten Cage's marriage. It was as mercifully brief as this bio: Cage ran from his wife and took up with a male dancer. As I was saying before, "Nut screws and bolts."

One obscure tidbit about Cage – come to think of it, every tidbit about Cage is obscure – is the fact that he was asked by Burgess 'The Penguin' Meredith to compose a documentary film score on Alexander Calder – the artist who made mobiles into 'kinetic sculpture.' My only thought on this is an equally obscure one: 'Bat-mobiles.'

Cage was best known for harnessing silence. His infamous composition *4'.33"* is a work for piano in which the pianist sits for four minutes and thirty-three seconds and doesn't play a note. There are many recordings of this work from which to choose, and I'm at a loss as to which one is the finer. At least Cage wrote a work that calls for the slamming shut of the piano lid. His pianos may have been prepared, but his audiences were not: Now they knew when it was time to wake up and go home.

Benjamin Britten
b. Lowestoft, England, 1913; d. Aldeburgh, England, 1976

Britten was born on St. Cecilia's day – the patron saint of music – so he wasn't allowed to become anything but a good composer. He started piano lessons at seven and begged to study a string instrument. *Voila!* His parents bought him a viola, upon which he became extremely adroit, *et à gauche* (ambidextrous, in fact – but I'll touch on sexuality later).

His parents were quick to recognize his musical gifts and sent him to study with a London Bridge. Dr. Frank Bridge looked at one of the boy's fresh compositions and asked him if what he had written was what he meant. When Britten replied in the affirmative, Bridge snapped, "Well, it ought not to have been." Britten, never one to cross a bridge until he got there, went on to write *Variations on a Theme by Bridge* – which contained just enough suspension to hold it in place. Some performers opt for the abridged version.

Another teacher of Britten's was John Ireland. As his name implies, he was usually too waterlogged with Guinness to give this prize student his appointed harmony lesson, and Britten thought his diet was making him too stout – or perhaps he meant his diet was two stout. At any rate, Britten wanted the Royal College of Music to send him to Austria to study with Alban Berg. The RCM told Ben's parents Berg had dubious qualities and would not be a good example. The mere mention of 'atonality' and 'homophonic tendencies' made the couple forbid their little innocent from visiting this Viennese composer with the artistic licentiousness.

Britten went on to meet the likes of Auden, Waugh, Isherwood and Peter Pears. It is apparent in his recent biographies that Benjamin Britten must have been a very heavy sleeper. Auden tried awakening him several times, but he was never really aroused unless Peter Pears was around. He had met Pears in 1937 and fell in love with his voice. From that point on, Pears sang Britten's praises, premiering every tenor role with a kind of nasal strangulation (but always *musically* strangulated).

In 1938, Britten bought an old mill and turned its circularroom into a very tasteful music study – which explains

why he never seemed to write himself into a corner. While returning to England from America in 1942, he composed *Hymn to St. Cecilia* on a ship while sitting next to a humming refrigerator. The appliance droned a continuous 'E' which became the work's tonal centre, placing St. Cecilia in the fridgian mode. (Or was she in the *frigidian* mode?)

Hail Brittania! Britten woos the raves! This was certainly the case when the reviews were in for *Peter Grimes*, his operatic masterpiece. England was finally back on track as a country that could write indigenous opera, after only 200 years. Britten and Pears had moved to a seaside town called Aldeburgh, where he wrote the work in 1945. *Peter (Pears) Grimes* is the story of a mad fisherman who makes the entire borough suspicious of his dealings with boy apprentices. Another opera, *Turn of the Screw*, is the story of a governess who is suspicious of Peter (Pears) Quint and his dealings with Miles, the boy she is looking after. Britten obviously understood boy's voices and proved to be very adept at handling them – the voices that is.

Living by the sea and writing about it proved to be fertile ground for Britten. There are the famous *Sea Interludes* from *Peter Grimes*; *Billy Budd*, an all-male opera, where the action takes place on a ship; *Noyes Fludde*, the story of the ark; *Sammy's Bath* from *The Little Sweep*. With all that water vividly sloshing around in his music, it's no wonder there are noticeably longer lineups for the washrooms after a Britten concert.

Flash forward to 1962. Britten's monumental *War Requiem* is a watershed (although it takes place on land) of the composer's style and technique. It expresses his undying pacifism and the futility of war. And man, is it loud! The brass and percussion aren't so bad, but just wait for that screeching soprano to come in with *Rex Tremendae*. (If ever a war needs to be ended quickly, just send in 100,000 sopranos at full throttle.)

It was a crime in England to be anything but heterosexual until 1971, therefore Britten was denied a knighthood. England felt guilty after Britten died and made Peter Pears a 'Sir', but had trouble explaining his partner's relinquished award without appearing too surreptitious. The excuse Britain finally gave Pears: "We didn't want to appear too sir repetitious."

Arvo Part
b. Paide, Estonia, 1935

Pärt is a minimalist.

Arvo Part
b. Paide, Estonia, 1935

Pärt is a minimalist.

About the Author

Kevin Reeves is known as a true 'Renaissance Man' (he enjoys living in the past). He is currently working on two documentaries in the capacity of director and co-producer for his award-winning company, Zephyrus Productions Ltd. He is also writing an opera based on the story of Grey Owl, and contemplatting his next book, which may encompass the hystery of singers. Speaking of which, Reeves is director of *Seventeen Voyces* – an Ottawa-based chamber choir that specializes in Baroque music. He has been known to tackle contemporary composers as well, and has offered them rubbing alcohol and bandages in order to stop the bleeding. *The Composers* follows hot on the heels of his first book *Artoons: The Hystery of Art*, which was published by Sound And Vision in 1985. At that time, Reeves was a cartoonist with the Toronto Star, for which he created the panel *Limelight*, a satirical look at Canadians in the entertainment business. Reeves is still upset over that fateful day he was laid off at the Star (something to do with a *verboten* switch by the printing presses) and he hopes everything is going well in the new building.

The Composers: A Hystery of Music

First published in Canada by
Sound And Vision
359 Riverdale Avenue,
Toronto, Canada, M4J 1A4

http://www.soundandvision.com
E-mail: musicbooks@soundandvision.com

First printing, October 1998
1 3 5 7 9 11 13 15 - printings - 14 12 10 8 6 4 2

Canadian Cataloguing in Publication Data

Reeves, Kevin, 1958-
The Composers: a hystery of music
ISBN 0-920151-29-9
1. Composers – Caricatures 2. Composers – Biography.
I. Title.
ML390.R33 1998   780'.92'2   C98-932307-2

Jacket designed by Jim Stubbington

Typeset in Century Schoolbook
Printed and bound in Canada

Other books published by Sound And Vision

How to Stay Awake
During Anybody's Second Movement
by David E.Walden
preface by Charlie Farquharson
cartoons by Mike Duncan
isbn 0-920151-20-5

I Wanna Be Sedated
Pop Music in the Seventies
by Phil Dellio & Scott Woods
preface by Chuck Eddy
cartoons by Dave Prothero
isbn 0-920151-16-7

Love Lives of the Great Composers
From Gesualdo to Wagner
by Basil Howitt
cover by Dave Donald
isbn 0-920151-18-3

A Working Musician's Joke Book
by Daniel G. Theaker
preface by David W. Barber
cartoons by Mike Freen
isbn 0-920151-23-X

Artoons
The Hystery of Art
by Kevin Reeves
preface by Jim Unger
isbn 0-920151-05-1

Driving
The best means of picking up groceries, kids, egos,
speeding tickets and members of the opposite sex
by Stephen Barnes
isbn 0-920151-09-4

by David W. Barber and cartoons by Dave Donald

A Musician's Dictionary
preface by Yehudi Menuhin
isbn 0-920151-21-3

Bach, Beethoven and the Boys
Music History as It Ought to Be Taught
preface by Anthony Burgess
isbn 0-920151-10-8

When the Fat Lady Sings
Opera History as It Ought to Be Taught
preface by Maureen Forrester
isbn 0-920151-11-6

If it Ain't Baroque
More Music History as It Ought to Be Taught
isbn 0-920151-15-9

Getting a Handel on Messiah
preface by Trevor Pinnock
isbn 0-920151-17-5

Tenors, Tantrums and Trills
An Opera Dictionary from Aida to Zzzz
isbn 0-920151-19-1

TuTus, Tights and Tiptoes
Ballet History as It Ought to Be Taught
isbn 0-920151-30-2

by David W. Barber

Better Than It Sounds
A Dictionary of Humorous Musical Quotations
cover by Jim Stubbington
isbn 0-920151-22-1

Note from the Publisher

If you have any comments on this book or any other books we publish, or if you would like a catalogue, please write to us at Sound And Vision 359 Riverdale Avenue, Toronto, Canada M4J1A4. Or visit our web site at http://www.soundandvision. com.

We are always looking for original books to publish. If you have an idea or manuscript that is in the genre of musical humour, please contact us at our address above. Thank you for purchasing or *borrowing* this book!